Master Classes in Education Series

Reflecting on School Management

Anne Gold and Jennifer Evans

UK   Falmer Press, 1 Gunpowder Square, London, EC4A 3DE
USA   Falmer Press, Taylor & Francis Inc., 325 Chestnut Street, 8th Floor,
        Philadelphia, PA 19007

© Anne Gold and Jennifer Evans 1998

First published in 1998

A catalogue record for this book is available from the British Library

ISBN 0 7507 0806 9 cased ✓
ISBN 0 7507 0805 0 paper

Library of Congress Cataloging-in-Publication Data are available on request

Cover design by Caroline Archer
Cover printed in Great Britain by Flexiprint Ltd., Lancing, East Sussex

Typeset in 10/12 pt Garamond by
Graphicraft Limited, Hong Kong

Printed in Great Britain by T.J. International Ltd., Padstow on paper which has a specified pH value on final paper manufacture of not less than 7.5 and is therefore 'acid free'.

Reflecting on School Management

Master Classes in Education Series

Series Editors: John Head, School of Education, Kings College, University of London and Ruth Merttens, School of Teaching Studies, University of North London

Working with Adolescents: Constructing Identity
John Head *Kings College, University of London*

Testing: Friend or Foe? The Theory and Practice of Assessment and Testing
Paul Black *Kings College, University of London*

Doing Research/Reading Research: A Mode of Interrogation for Education
Andrew Brown and Paul Dowling *both of the Institute of Education, University of London*

Educating the Other: Gender, Power and Schooling
Carrie Paechter *School of Education, The Open University*

Reflecting on School Management
Anne Gold and Jennifer Evans *both of the Management Development Centre Institute of Education, University of London*

Contents

List of Figures and Tables

To Tibor and Alex

Series Editor's Preface

It has become a feature of our times that an initial qualification is no longer seen to be adequate for lifelong work within a profession and programmes of professional development are needed. Nowhere is the need more clear than with respect to education, where changes in the national schooling and assessment system, combined with changes in the social and economic context, have transformed our professional lives.

The series, *Master Classes in Education*, is intended to address the needs of professional development, essentially at the level of taught masters degrees. Although aimed primarily at teachers and lecturers, it is envisaged that the books will appeal to a wider readership, including those involved in professional educational management, health promotion and youth work. For some, the texts will serve to up-date their knowledge. For others, they may facilitate career reorientation by introducing, in an accessible form, new areas of expertise or knowledge.

The books are overtly pedagogical, providing a clear track through the topic by means of which it is possible to gain a sound grasp of the whole field. Each book familiarizes the reader with the vocabulary and the terms of discussion, and provides a concise overview of recent research and current debates in the area. While it is obviously not possible to deal with every aspect in depth, a professional who has read the book should be able to feel confident that they have covered the major areas of content, and discussed the different issues at stake. The books are also intended to convey a sense of the future direction of the subject and its points of growth or change.

In each subject area the reader is introduced to different perspectives and to a variety of readings of the subject under consideration. Some of the readings may conflict, others may be compatible but distant. Different perspectives may well give rise to different lexicons and different bibliographies, and the reader is always alerted to these differences. The variety of frameworks within which each topic can be construed is then a further source of reflective analysis.

The authors in this series have been carefully selected. Each person is an experienced professional, who has worked in that area of education as a practitioner and also addressed the subject as a researcher and theoretician. Drawing upon both pragmatic and the theoretical aspects of their experience, they are able to take a reflective view while preserving a sense of what occurs, and what is possible, at the level of practice.

Reflecting on School Management

No where has change been more marked in education than in the increase in managerial responsibilities now placed on senior teachers. The transfer of functions, including control of the school budget, from Local Education Authorities to individual schools has created an entirely new set of concerns for school staff and governors. At least two problems have made the situation particularly difficult.

We have had until recently no career structure for teachers to enter into these management posts. It was assumed that the experienced and successful classroom teacher could automatically take on the additional duties. A contrast can be drawn with the common pattern in the United States where career paths for teachers diverge after a few years of professional experience and some elect to leave the classroom, and through study and acting as 'administrative interns' within a school equip themselves for managerial responsibilities. The speed of change within Britain following the 1988 Education Reform Act caught the profession unprepared.

The second problem is that we lacked a theory or model of school management. As a consequence models drawn from industry and commerce were often intro-duced to fill the vacancy, although it is not clear how applicable these notions might be to the new setting. Ideas of profit, efficiency and of the customer have question-able significance to schools. The concept of the market has been introduced through increased parental choice but many of the market disciplines and procedures do not prevail. Consequently a new generation of academics have had to define and de-velop models of what school management might and should entail.

The authors of this book have been in the forefront of this development, run-ning a successful taught masters degree programme at the Institute of Education in London. This book is based on the insights gained from the experience of working on the course and represents the state of the art in this field.

John Head and Ruth Merttens
Series Editors

Introduction

We are course leaders of and contributors to MAs in Education Management at the Institute of Education, University of London. In our teaching, we are used to laying theoretical frameworks about management in education before our students and then engaging with them in critical questioning in order to contest and critique the different frameworks we have offered.

We work with teachers and managers from many countries to fit their professional experiences of schools into and around the theories we are examining, and we offer readings and research findings to make sense of their professional worlds and to plan for any necessary changes. We are clear, both to ourselves and with students, that different theoretical frameworks work for different situations. We try to be non-judgmental, although discerning readers of this book will probably be able to work out our beliefs about management in education. We hope we allow those with whom we argue to work with their own beliefs. Our main expectation is that those beliefs are clearly articulated.

The principal challenge for us in writing this book was to endeavour to capture the excitement and the discussion that we enjoy in the interactions in our classrooms. We have written a book which is intended to talk to, to engage with and to challenge the reader. The boxed tasks are planned to give readers the opportunity to reflect — they are to replace that silence in class that comes after we ask: 'well, what do *you* think?' The tasks are designed to help readers to come to their own conclusions about the different conceptual frameworks offered, and to draw out their own implications for policy and practice. We hope they do so in a dynamic and stimulating way. This is not a calm and measured book partly because management in education is not a calm and measured activity, and partly because good learning is not usually calm and measured.

Many books on management in education suggest clear and simply structured systems, implying that all management problems will be solved when the right strategy is chosen. Indeed, managers may well have a sense of failure after working through such books, because they often do not take into account the people and the contexts to be managed. The people with whom they work may not have read the same texts, and may not wish to be managed by such systems. We hope that readers of this book will develop their *own* management styles based on and informed by the knowledge described here, rather than adopt unquestioningly carefully prescribed models.

We chose the title of our book after much discussion and reflection because we wanted to make it clear that the opportunity to reflect on management practice, the chance to combine that reflection with new knowledge, the space to plan for changes in practice, and then the opportunity to reflect on the new practice are all at the heart of educative management and of a learning school. We tried to write a book which planned for and encouraged all these stages in learning to take place. The contrast between the busy working lives that teachers in the United Kingdom (UK) lead and the active reflection that is known to make for best professional practice is quite disturbing. In a small way, we hope that this book will allow those two ends of the spectrum to come closer together.

This book is full of quotations from and references to other writers for two reasons:

1   we have tried to select interesting and stimulating passages as tasters and introductions to other readings with full references, so that someone using this book as a basic text about school management will have enough evidence to decide which further reading might be helpful;
2   the readings are an attempt by us to introduce new conceptual frameworks and research findings in order to help the reader make sense of reflections on practice and to make plans for different professional practice if necessary.

Chapter 1 introduces a reflective dimension immediately by setting up thought-provoking themes which recur throughout the book. In it, we invite readers to think about the values that underpin school management. We discuss some ethical dimensions to school management and show how these are linked to understandings of leadership, power and values. We then ask how principles of democracy, choice, power and equity might impact on the management of education in the current context.

In Chapter 2, we link the shared articulation of the purpose of a school with its culture and ethos, and ask how organizational structures are informed by and impact on the published values of the school. Organizational structures and decision-making routes are both visible and invisible signifiers of a school's ethos and values, and make clear signals to all who work there about the value of their contributions to the direction of the school.

Chapter 3 attempts to answer basic questions such as the meaning of 'management', 'leadership', and 'administration'. It introduces several theories about management and leadership styles, and briefly touches on the quality movement and on 'educative management'. It draws attention to the importance of a manager having an understanding of how teams and team building work: we think that this understanding is closely linked with certain management and leadership styles.

Chapter 4 deals with a set of management skills. This chapter may read very differently from most of the other chapters in the book because it *does* offer some strategies for managing. We hope, though, that each time we do so, we offer both a selection of different possibilities and some underpinning questions so that the strategies cannot be adopted unquestioningly. We divide the chapter into two sections:

self and system management skills which includes managing time, decision making, and strategic planning;
and *managing with other people* which includes managing conflict, working with difficult people, motivation, delegation, and managing stress.

Chapter 5 is also about working with people, but here the focus is on developing staff. The key word in this chapter is 'developing', and we work through three case studies in order to examine such continuing professional development issues as: who the term 'staff' includes; staff selection and recruitment, staff induction, notions of continuing professional development, appraisal, and the Human Resource Management approach.

In Chapter 6, we look at the external context for school management in the UK in the late twentieth century, and we offer some key points that we hope managers can bear in mind when managing schools in the education market place. We give a guide to the legislative framework for school managers, explain some of the problems and possibilities to be found in the education market, look at the impact of the market on education and remind readers about equity, social responsibility and education.

Chapter 7 invites the reader to think about some of the issues underpinning the management of finances and resources. Once again, we ask about power balances and about the values underpinning the financial decisions made in a school. After describing the legislative framework, and going through the budgetary process, we ask questions about good financial management. We have introduced a case study here to allow the reader to make some decisions about budgeting and resources which are informed by the guidelines we draw up earlier in the chapter.

Chapter 8 looks at the interface between the school and outside agencies. We explain the concept of 'stakeholders', and then write about parental involvement. In the UK, many governors do not appear to have understood their full responsibilities towards the schools they govern, so we suggest some of the issues to be borne in mind while managing with governors. The role of the Local Education Authority (LEA), the Office for Standards in Education (OfSTED), *vis-à-vis* schools seem to be constantly changing and regularly contested. We discuss the role of the local community and refer to professional help for schools, using this chapter generally to set the school within the context of stakeholders.

Chapter 9 looks back into the school, and explores the management of learning and teaching. We begin by defining 'curriculum' and trying to ascertain whose responsibility it is to manage it. We go on to look at curriculum planning, the influence of the school culture and values on the curriculum and how these may be linked. We discuss the responsibility for planning and delivering the curriculum and suggest some basic principles that might underpin the monitoring and evaluating of curriculum delivery.

Beryl Husain's contribution to our thinking has been invaluable. Many of the activities suggested in this book are a result of our creative and practical collaboration over several years.

Janet Ouston has written Chapter 10 and we think that it encapsulates both the dynamism and the turbulence of school management at this time in the UK. Janet writes about turbulence and then shows ways of managing change within that turbulence. She offers a wide-ranging and knowledgeable review of relevant literature, some helpful frameworks for managing change in these times, and finally reminds all managers of the importance of clear and visible values.

We should like to thank all the teachers and school managers we work with and have worked with. They are at least half the equation that has allowed us to develop the ideas and questions we have written about in this book. Without their questions and their grounding of some of our more bizarre ideas in the reality of everyday school life, the conceptual frameworks offered here may have made no sense at all. At least this way, we hope they will make some sense.

Anne Gold and Jennifer Evans
London, January 1998

Chapter 1

Philosophy and Values in Education Management

This chapter introduces some ideas and questions which give strength and support to explorations of school management by setting them within an ethical dimension. Throughout the chapter, there is a comparative and international perspective that we would like to introduce as a sub-theme throughout the book.

Key issues for managers:

- The importance of the articulation of underlying principles;

- The need for an ethical approach to management in education;

- Issues of democracy, choice, power and equal opportunities;

- Managing current contexts according these principles.

Educational Principles and Values

The Collins English Dictionary (1990) defines 'ethical' as:

> *adj.* 1. of or based on a system of moral beliefs about right and wrong. 2. in accordance with principles of professional conduct.

These two definitions link an understanding of right and wrong with notions of professionalism. Teachers are sometimes uncomfortable about the use of the term 'professional' in relation to their work. For some, it signifies a depth of reflection and understanding about taking responsibility for the activities of learning and teaching which is underpinned by years of involvement in and commitment to education. In other words for them, each action taken and all decisions made about every aspect of learning and teaching are based on a clearly articulated set of ethically based beliefs and understandings about the purpose of education.

Other teachers remember with discomfort what Grace (1987) calls 'the legitimated professionalism which emerged in the 1930s'. This professionalism

> involved an understanding that organised teachers would keep to their proper sphere of activity within the classroom and the educational system and the state, for its part, would grant them a measure of trust, a measure of material reward and occupational security, and a measure of professional dignity. (p. 208)

For these teachers, a mistrust of the term 'professional' comes from what they see as a historical narrowing and limiting of their sphere of action. For many years after the 1930s, this narrowness seemed to disappear to reflect more the first definition of professionalism. But the Education Reform Act of 1988 was initially so prescriptive that it made teachers begin to question once again British society's expectations about their autonomy and professionalism. Does a truly professional body work to such clearly *externally* prescribed guidelines? It remains to be seen where the British government and British society of the late twentieth and early twenty-first centuries position teachers. Who will continue to decide what is taught in British schools and how it will be taught? Whose values and ethics will teachers be working with in schools?

At present, the Department for Education and Employment (DfEE) expects that schools will include a statement about their educational values in their documentation. They may call it their mission statement, or the school's vision of education, their values statement, their beliefs about education, their school's statement of purpose or their school aims. However they describe it, it is that which makes each school different from any other, but only if it is put into operation within and around the school. In other words, the managers of a school have a responsibility to see that the values stated are implicit in every activity that takes place in the school. For example, many schools include in their statement such phrases as 'enriching' or 'achieve potential' or 'recognizing and celebrating differences'. Are these values communicated clearly to a visitor or a stranger walking round the school? Chapter 2 explores this issue in more detail, and follows on to show how the school's declared purpose will be agreed and clearly articulated, so that the published purpose informs the culture of the school. Here, however, it is important to note that a statement of principles or values from each school is expected by law.

In what way are these values ethical? What is the connection between values and ethics, and why must those who manage schools ensure that their management decisions have an ethical basis? Robert J. Starratt (1996) writes:

> While it includes conversations with individual teachers, the larger work of administration involves calling all the teachers to the building of an ethical school. This involvement provides the administrator and the teachers with a large moral task, one that will never be finished, but one that will enable them to integrate many of the specific moral and professional components of teaching into a larger, meaningful whole. One might benignly interpret all or much that teachers presently do as tacitly involved with nurturing an ethical school. In the best of schools that may certainly be true. I suggest that they do this work more intentionally, discussing explicitly the fundamental components of the task and seeking through explicit programmatic elements to offer an intentional environment for moral learning. (p. 156)

Starratt builds up his argument by explaining that ethics is the *study* of moral practice, and as a scholarly inquiry 'ethics tends to dissect human actions, thinking, and choices in order to understand when they are ethical or unethical'. Thus, those who are involved in ethical school management, and the management of ethical schools, must ensure that there are spaces for reflection, for conversations and for planning during the school day. These spaces will offer teachers the opportunity to 'study' and think about practice, in order to plan consciously for ethical interactions.

There is a danger in schools that those working in them take for granted that there is only one true set of values. Bottery (1992) writes:

> values may be contested within an organization, and values not necessarily in accord with those passed down the hierarchy may be adopted and practised by those within the organization. Values, then, cannot be simply held as objectively correct, but are adopted for particular purposes by particular people or groups, and are therefore contestable. (pp. 180–181)

This quotation raises an interesting management question: a principled school manager may believe that those who work in the school should have space to develop and work with their own educational values. But the same manager is committed to embedding the school's published purpose in all that happens there — how might the different sets of values be mediated? Or indeed, is there room for different sets of values in one educational organization?

It might be helpful here to think about the values underpinning the organization in which you are working. The following set of questions could be answered in conjunction with the questionnaire in Chapter 2, in which it is suggested that the school ethos reflects the values of the school.

Activity

Tracking the Values System within a School

First attempt to answer the following questions alone, and then, if appropriate, compare your answers with those of a colleague within your school with whom you believe you share values.

1   Without reference to any school literature or publications, write down what you remember of the school statement of values.

2   Check what you have written with the statement published in literature about the school.

3   What do you think a senior manager in your school might write if asked the same question?

4   What do you think a very new teacher might write if asked the same question?

5   What do you think a pupil would answer?

6   What might a parent say?

7   What would a member of support staff in your school say?

8   And what might a visitor to the school say after spending half an hour on the premises?

If the values in a school are clearly shared and articulated, then most of the answers to the above questions would be the same. All the constituencies with a stake in the educational organization will have had an input into the formation of the statement, and will have contributed to its regular review, or will have made a conscious choice to be involved in the organization because the statement matches their own values.

If, however, they are not shared, the answers may be very different. And does this matter? If, as Bottery (1992) writes, values may be contested within an organization, how might different contexts affect their articulation of values in one organization?

Ethical Dimensions to School Management

One arena in which values are clearly affected by different contexts is the management or leadership style employed by the headteacher and other managers. This is examined in greater detail in Chapter 3, but in order to begin to explore the links between leadership and values, here is a very simple summary of a continuum of leadership styles. Based on the ethical beliefs of the headteacher, it might encompass the following ways of managing:

Autocratic ↔ Paternalistic ↔ Consultative ↔ Democratic ↔ Abdicatory
(Tell)   (Sell)   (Involve)   (Co-determine) (Give up)

In order to help make sense of this continuum, you might think about your own management style and about your response to the management styles of others.

Activity

After thinking about your own understanding of management values, place yourself on the continuum above, then answer the following questions:

1 Which style(s) do *you* respond to?
2 Which style encourages teamwork?
3 Which style is nearest to your own dominant styles?
4 Are leaders always consistent in their styles? If not, why not?

The answer to the fourth question left will probably include such circumstances as:

- it depends on the task to be managed;
- it depends on who is to be managed;
- it depends on the understanding and commitment to the task of those who are to be managed;
- it depends on the resources;
- it depends on external demands;
- it depends on the time allowed to manage the task and
- it depends on the educational and management principles of the manager.

It is probably true, however, that apart from the times when autocratic management is imperative (such as in times of immediate danger, when commands are non-negotiable), most leaders hover around one point on the continuum whatever answers they come to. They may waver depending on the answers above, and may at times feel driven towards managing in an alien style, but their fundamental beliefs about the purpose of education will inform the basic choice of leadership style. For example, a leader who believes absolutely in democracy and empowerment in education will work as often as possible in a democratic way with other teachers and members of the school, encouraging them, perhaps, to develop and use an informed voice in decision-making.

In this way, a headteacher who believes that all needs in the school community should be balanced as carefully as possible will base management decisions on the diagram introduced by John Adair (1986) (*Figure 1.1*) in which he shows that teams work best when attention is paid equally to three sets of needs:

Figure 1.1: Effective teambuilding

Source: ADAIR, J. (1986) *Effective Teambuilding*, Reading: Pan

Should one set of needs — say an individual teacher's need — overpower the needs of the institution or the task, the task of education within the school will not easily be achieved. Should the demands of the task overshadow the needs of individuals within the school, there will be depression, stress and general disquiet. And should the needs of the institution take precedence over the needs of the individual and the task, unhappy teachers will not be able to ensure that the young people in the school are receiving the education that the school has stated as its purpose. The initial recognition of the necessity to balance the needs, and then the definition or measure of the different balances will all depend on the headteacher's educational and management values, and therefore the management choices made. To what extent does the definition of balance — the power to encourage such decisions about a school and its values — reside with the headteacher?

Leadership, Power and Values

Hodgkinson (1991) argues that although a leader has structural or executive power coming from the formal legal structure, 'power in another sense always rests ultimately with the individual components of that structure' (p. 80). He goes on to say that those people who are managed can find ways of refusing to do what their manager wishes them to do — they can always quit, walk away or sabotage. And he writes that part of a leader's skill is to be able to persuade followers to follow. These leadership skills are the ones he sees as political skills:

The intimate connection between power, political power (itself a value), and the resolution of common problems emphasizes the necessity for the educational leader to have political skills and to be, in part at least, a politician. This in itself, of course, entails no guarantee of ethical responsibility; it only recognizes that without under- standing of and access to the hierarchy of political decision-making, ethical respons- ibility may simply be impossible. (p. 37)

The values implicit in political understandings of management become more obvious in writings about discourses. Such writings explore the political and the micropolitical aspects of organizational management by looking at dominant belief systems and the ways that they are transmitted. Decision-making and micropolitics in schools are examined further in Chapter 2, so here, more attention is paid to prevailing discourses in schools. Ball (1990) explains the concept of 'discourses' as identified by Foucault:

> Discourses are about what can be said and what can be thought, but also about who can speak, when, and with what authority. Discourses embody meaning and social relations, they constitute both subjectivity and power relations . . . Thus the possibilities for meaning and for definition, are pre-empted through the social and institutional position held by those who use them. (p. 2)

So, when those who are managed feel less powerful than those who manage them because of their formal position within the structure of the organization; when the dominant discourses about learning and teaching within the school are not in tune with their own; when they are asked to take part in whole-school activities for which they have repugnance or dislike, it is not as easy as Hodgkinson asserts to 'quit, walk away or sabotage'. The dominant discourses are often so powerful that the dissenter finds it hard to voice dissent articulately or objectively, and the over- powering manager uses the strength of their discourse to silence that dissent. A more ethical manager may wish to encourage informed debate by giving space to different positions, and thus incorporating them all into a larger and stronger whole.

Some of the traditional sites of power within organizations are dependent on the official structure of the organization, on the history and traditions of the organ- ization, or on the external values given to the organization's activities. In the UK in the late twentieth century, these sites of power might translate in the following ways:

- *The official structure of the organization* becomes the formal hierarchy within a school: a headteacher or a senior teacher in a school traditionally has more decision-making power than a pupil or a newly qualified teacher.

- *The history and traditions of the organization* make change very difficult and schools change-resistant: newcomers and suggestions for new ways of doing things are often met with 'that's not how we do things here!'

- *The external values given to the organization's activities* are epitomized by the public contestation of the legitimacy of different types of league tables of results: different schools are successively positioned as failing or succeeding depending on the way the information about their work is publicized. And ultimately schools succeed or fail because of the numbers of parents who choose to send their children to be educated by them — in the market place, those schools which do not have sufficient pupils (and thus resourcing) will close.

But the power which is harder to discern, which is legitimated within hard-to-read discourses, and which, when managed ethically, makes for a learning and constantly developing school, is the real focus for ethical managers. They know that an understanding of that power and the effects of it on other people is of the greatest importance. All learning, for young people and for adults, depends on the learner feeling safe and even powerful enough to take risks and to make mistakes (which can then be reflected on for learning for the future). It is here that learning and management come very close to each other: those people who are managed in such a way as to feel powerful and effective are more likely to make sure that the learning and teaching for which they have responsibility will empower learners.

However, European society is structured in such a way as to ensure various overlapping sites of initial disadvantage and disempowerment. Western European society privileges those who are adult male, white, middle-class, able-bodied and heterosexual. So, women, children, people from ethnic minorities, working-class, aged, homosexual and disabled people do not naturally have access to positions of power or decision-making: they usually have to struggle harder to find a voice. And if they come from multiple sites of disadvantage — women from ethnic minorities, or working-class and disabled men, for example — their attempts to have access to cultural capital or the normal resources of a 'developed' society are even more fraught with difficulty. This positioning is often very subtle and hard to articulate — strong discourses of normality prevail which compound and reconfirm marginalization. Those who are marginalized often do not realize that they are disempowered — the strength of the discourse is such that many exclusions from power are taken for granted as natural. An ethical headteacher is aware of this, for both staff and students in a school, and will take steps to empower those who are societally disadvantaged.

Activity

Sites of power and disempowerment in your school

This activity will help you think about the access to power for both learners and teachers in your school.

1 In one column, list all the possible sites of disempowerment that **the young people** in your school might experience — race, class, gender, poverty, sexual preference, size, disability, etc.

2 Rank the sites in order of significant impact on learning, giving each site a score out of ten which indicates the size of the disadvantage.

3 In another column next to the first column, begin the same process again with **members of staff**, this time using official positions within the school hierarchy as the social class indicator.

4 Compare the two columns. Are the outcomes of your staff list a surprise to you?

5 Is the staff column anything like the column that you have drawn up for pupils?

6 What sort of modelling of positions of power within the school does the staff offer the young people?

How might a headteacher become ethically aware in this way? The statistics about secondary school headteachers in Western Europe show that most of them come from positions of social advantage — they are most likely to be white middle-class men. However, the young people in their schools increasingly come from ethnic minorities, and the teachers in their schools are as likely to be women as men (and more likely to be women in primary schools).

Most people who have felt less than powerful at some stage in their lives, and have realized that they were feeling powerless, find it easier to understand the effects of disempowering management styles. They know at first hand what disempowerment feels like. But knowledge and understanding are not enough. Rather like Kolb's learning cycle (1984), it is necessary to have a reflective intervention, and also to have the opportunity to plan to do things differently. In other words, it is important to *understand* the effects of disempowerment, then to articulate a set of principles to alleviate those effects, and to develop strategies to put those principles into practice. People who work through all of these stages — feeling (or observing empathetically) the effects of the misuse of power; reflecting upon those effects; drawing up principles which counteract those effects; putting strategies in place based on the principles; then observing to see whether the strategies work to empower rather than disempower — are most likely to work with 'power for', rather than 'power over'. They are most likely to be the ones who work towards what Shirley Grundy (1993) calls 'emancipatory praxis.'

Having either experienced or empathetically understood disempowerment, and having reflected on the effects of disempowerment on the autonomy of someone who is managed in this way, the empowering leader will manage in a way that will encourage autonomy in others. In other words, they will use the power invested in them by virtue of their management position to empower those they manage to work autonomously, creatively and productively.

It is clear that some men who fit all these categories do not manage in a patriarchal way. And when women, or people who come from other sites of apparent or potential disadvantage, reach positions of power, they do not always work in an empowering and collaborative way. So, what makes the difference? How have these people interrupted the inevitability of managing in pre-ordained ways? It is clear that managers who have understood the effects of power and have chosen to manage empoweringly will find themselves functioning like the women headteachers in Valerie Hall's (1996) research:

A picture emerges of women heads enacting strong leadership within a collaborative framework. In spite of this, the women heads . . . were firmly committed to the belief that sharing leadership still required them to take the lead when appropriate, including having a personal vision for the school. They saw themselves (and were seen) as key players, co-ordinating, developing and using others' efforts to the benefit of the school's purpose. (p. 190)

Managing Current Contexts According to Principles of Democracy, Choice, Power and Equal Opportunities

Most of this chapter has focused on managing internally — ethical managers understand the effects of their management actions on those they manage, and pay constant attention to in-school power balances. However, the education market place has introduced competition and rivalry between schools, especially where there are more school places than students within one locality. Chapter 6 explores the legislative framework that has been introduced to encourage market place tactics between schools and raises problems and possibilities within this paradigm. Here, however, we wish to remind those with responsibility for managing schools that they might decide not to be automatically competitive with other local schools. Ethical managers must remind their stakeholders about the equitable approach to education they have agreed within the educational values of the school, and show how these can be encouraged between schools as well as within them. They need to find a balance between making sure that their school survives, and working collaboratively for the good of the community. This means that they have to operate effectively but also ethically within the current competitive environment. This issue is explored further in Chapter 6.

> **Activity**
> What are the external contexts for power and equity in which Valerie Hall's headteachers are working, and how might those contexts affect the work in their schools at present?

Equal Opportunities Policies and Equity

Some European countries have equal opportunities legislation. Some schools have equal opportunities policies, but policies are not always carried out in practice, and laws are not always upheld. In the 1980s in the UK, most schools developed and adopted equal opportunities policies, and even appointed named teachers as equal opportunities post holders. There was support for this work from local education authorities, who provided resources to develop such work. It soon became apparent, however, that initially, responsibility for equal opportunities was left to rest with the post holder, and only in exceptional schools did practice change for everyone. In some schools, those who had responsibility for the marginalized were made to feel marginalized themselves, and their activities and suggestions were received as if they came from their own private enterprise. Once this positioning was perceived and understood, most people working in schools in the UK began to share responsibility for equity and very exciting and innovative work took place. Changes were made in recruitment practices, in staffroom ethos and in school ethos generally, and in the classroom, expectations were changed about learning and teaching in particular.

In the 1990s, with the introduction of external constraints such as league tables of results, grant maintained status for schools, and the putting in place of the education market-place, local education authorities have not found it as easy to encourage such attention to equal opportunities procedures, and many individual schools have used their freedom from central government to loosen such controls. There is no local government monitoring of admission procedures to grant maintained schools, and many schools are reluctant to take in young people whose special needs or whose general lack of access to the cultural capital will lower the school's place in the results league tables.

There are, however, many schools which do much more than pay lip-service to notions of equity, and which empower and encourage learning and teaching from all parts of the school community. One aspect of the proposed reformulation of the league tables is an insistence on an awareness of the different sites of disadvantage which affect the make up of a school's community, and an insistence that the school's attempts to compensate for these sites are taken into account and celebrated where relevant. Hence it is necessary to return to the school leadership's articulation of educational values which take account of the need to recognize all learners' and teachers' previous access to power while making plans to empower them to continue learning.

Conclusion

Strong links have been made between educational values and the evidence of equitable practices within a school. The headteacher's understanding of and commitment to the empowerment of learners will have a direct effect both on those learners in the school and on the way the school is managed. The educational philosophy and values of those who manage a school will inform the management styles chosen and will help the managers to mediate the external context of education with the agreed purpose of the school.

Understanding about power and empowerment is encouraged by those who manage the teaching and learning in equitable schools, and this understanding allows for strategies to compensate for initially disempowering backgrounds.

References

ADAIR, J. (1986) *Effective Teambuilding*, Reading: Pan.
BALL, S. (Ed) (1990) *Foucault and Education*, London: Routledge.
BOTTERY, M. (1992) *The Ethics of Educational Management*, London: Cassell.
COLLINS. (1990) *The Collins Paperback English Dictionary*, Glasgow: Harper Collins.
GRACE, G. (1987) 'Teachers and the state in Britain: A changing relation', in LAWN, M. and GRACE, G. *Teachers: The Culture and Politics of Work*, London: The Falmer Press.
GRUNDY, S. (1993) 'Educational leadership as emancipatory praxis', in BLACKMORE, J. and KENWAY, J. (Eds) *Gender Matters in Educational Administration and Policy*, London: Falmer Press.
HALL, V. (1996) *Dancing on the Ceiling*, London: Paul Chapman Publishing.
HODGKINSON, C. (1991) *Educational Leadership: The Moral Art*, Albany: State University of New York Press.
KOLB, D. (1984) *Experiential Learning*, New Jersey: Prentice-Hall.
STARRATT, R. (1996) *Transforming Educational Administration*, USA: McGraw-Hill.

Chapter 2

What Is Management in Education?

This chapter explores the importance of the clear articulation of a school's purpose of education and the links between its stated educational philosophy and the way the school is organized to allow for teaching and learning. It goes on to connect the purpose of a school with the culture of the school and its effect on the pupils who learn there. It then traces the organizational structure chosen to the stated values and philosophy, reflects on the differences between middle and senior management, and asks who informs the management decisions in schools. Planned for decision-making processes are often subverted by micropolitical activity, and suggestions are made about the reasons why alternative power bases and decision-making routes develop. Questions are asked of school managers about whether to pay attention to or to ignore the micropolitics in their schools.

Key issues for managers:

- Articulating the purpose of the school;

- How the purpose of a school informs its culture;

- How organizational structures connect with the purpose of a school;

- Who informs the management decisions of a school?

- How are management decisions made in a school?

Articulating the Purpose of a School

It is important to think about this issue because the answer impacts on all the business carried on in schools. When teachers are asked why they work in education and what they see as the purpose of education, it is clear from the difficulty they often have in formulating their answers that they are not used to addressing these questions. But research, for example Barth (1990), Mortimore, Sammons, Stoll, Lewis and Ecob (1989), Bolam, McMahon, Pocklington and Weindling (1993), shows that a school where the purpose of education is clearly articulated and communicated is a far more effective school than one in which there is no obviously agreed purpose, or where the headteacher's view of education and schooling is not informed by and transmitted to the other people who work there.

A school's curriculum is predicated upon its purpose: before British state school-teachers' perceptions of a school curriculum and its content were more formally (and perhaps narrowly) defined by the National Curriculum, there was a generally shared understanding that 'curriculum' meant all the learning that went on in a school. Self-confident schools are aware of this and still pay attention to *all* the learning that takes place in the organization. Different writers describe the purpose of education differently, depending on their explanations of society. They are all aware that the ethos and culture that set the scene for learning are deeply affected by the management style, structure and activities of the headteacher. Per Dalin (1993) offers a framework for self-confident schools when he writes about a future for schooling in which he describes education in a way that reframes the way many people have come to think about schools:

1 *The paradigm shift*: The world is changing dramatically; we are in the middle of a major paradigm shift, and add-on changes to the existing schools are inadequate. Meaningful educational changes demand new perspectives and basic changes in the culture of schools.

2 *The school as the unit of change*: The school is the unit of change, because it is the only place where the demands of society and the expectations and learning needs of students and teachers meet. Each school is unique. It must learn how to learn.

3 *Central authorities as partners*: The school is part of nation-building. It is not alone; it needs the challenges and the support of central authorities. Many future problems are overwhelming and can only be dealt with as a result of close co-operation between the school and central authorities.

4 *The real needs*: School improvements, to be effective, must meet the real needs of students. To reach this goal is a complex process of developing ownership and a shared vision of short-term and long-term goals within each school.

5 *Change as learning*: Changes that have an impact on students' lives involve an in-depth learning process that can only be mastered by teachers and heads who themselves are learning, in teams that can draw on the talents of all members, and in the school as an organization involving all participants. Meaningful changes are dependent on *personal mastery* [sic], an outcome of a continuous process of learning (Senge, 1990).

6 *The learning organization*: The goal is a learning organization that is able to respond creatively to changes in the environment; an organization that has embedded capacities for school-based curriculum changes, for staff development and supervision, for team development as well as management and organizational development; and, not least, that has institutionalized the process of ongoing school assessment. (p. 2)

In other words, Per Dalin sees schooling as a highly socially responsible activity, where education is connected to society more openly and clearly than it often is at present. He describes a time when schools will overtly act as agents of social change, connecting national directions with the needs of students, mediated through support from central authority. *Everyone* is a learner in an effective school, and the school must be organized in such a way as to optimize everybody's learning. In order to create such a learning environment, most schools must introduce basic changes in culture.

His description of schooling has a familiar ring to teachers who entered the teaching profession in Western Europe and North America in the 1960s and 1970s, but few teachers nowadays formally admit to a wish to change society through their work. Dalin encourages the admission of such a principle, because it contributes to the ethos and culture of a school, and has an affect on the learning and management style of all the people who work there.

Paulo Freire, the Brazilian educator, had a revolutionary view of the purpose of education. Paul Taylor (1993) writes about Freire that

> on the one hand, he is asserting that education is a means of transforming reality, by which he means 'the social reality'. On the other hand he also insists that the education system, or at least 'radical change in the educational system', is contingent upon the radical transformation of society. (p. 53)

So Freire also sees education as an important tool of social change, but he has a much more radical view than Dalin about the linkage between education and society, and indeed between class and access to education.

Mortimore et al. (1989) in a very measured and careful book explain how their research showed that different schools had a marked and different effect on the attainment of their pupils:

> Our results indicate that the school to which a child belongs during the junior years can have a beneficial or negative effect on her or his progress and development. The importance of school in explaining variations in pupils' progress over the junior years is a major finding of this study. (p. 204)

These writings are introduced here to show that educationalists have many different views about the relationship between society and education, but none of them doubt that schooling and education have effects on the learners who attend schools that reach far beyond whether they are eventually literate and numerate. It is necessary, therefore, for those adults who work in schools to articulate and communicate their philosophy of education clearly to all the stakeholders of the school. It may be necessary for them to take into account the educational philosophies of the stakeholders and the whole community of the school when framing their philosophy. It is certainly necessary for those who lead schools to facilitate a communal description of schooling and the particular purpose of the school.

Begin by articulating your own philosophy here:

Activity
Answer this question in one or two sentences — **What do you see as the purpose of schooling?**

How Does the Purpose of a School Inform Its Culture?

It might be said that in a school where the purpose of education was clear, all visitors could 'read' the school's values on entering the building. For example, the entrance hall, while maintaining the safety of the people who work in the school, would give welcoming messages and would transmit an ethos of value for everybody: visitors would be warmly introduced to the learning environment of the school. The way that visitors are welcomed and asked about their business in the school, the representation of the children through their work or photographs of them, the status of the person who greets visitors (pupil, teacher, support staff or no-one), and the warmth, decor and cleanliness are all indicators of the ethos and culture of a school.

On walking further into the building, a visitor can initially see how a school values its members by looking at the ease or difficulty by which classrooms can be entered, by listening to the way teachers and children address each other, by watching how the children and staff use the communal spaces such as the corridors and the school hall, by looking at the work on display, by listening to the noise levels, and by hearing how requests for help or attention are responded to by teachers.

If a school professes in its statement of educational philosophy that it values all children as individuals and wishes to help them to attain their full potential (and most schools do say this in some form), then the reality of that statement can first be measured by the indicators already mentioned. If a school community goes on to express concern about notions of equity such as race, class and gender in the school aims, then the reality of those concerns should be clearly visible through criteria framed and publicized by the school's stakeholders. It may be for example, that these criteria result in:

- visible efforts to ensure the representation of staff and young people from ethnic minorities, women and girls, and working-class people in positions of decision-making within the school;

- information given about the activities the pupils go on to become involved in after leaving the school;

- celebration of the achievements of all young people in the school, not just the most academically able;

- careful attention given by staff to option and subject choices made by young people so that they do not become 'self-fulfilling prophesies'.

Nationally agreed success criteria for British schools are going through a re-definition by the state at the moment. Examination results, attendance records, and other statistics are published in the public domain. Schools which value less easily measurable outcomes of the learning and teaching processes (such as those listed above), as well as the futures of their children, have to struggle to legitimate their own, added, criteria unless they can persuade all concerned of the importance of the endeavour.

Activity

This checklist may be useful in helping teachers to think about how schools put principles about education into practice. It offers ways of thinking about how staff and pupils are valued and how the purpose of the organization permeates all the activities undertaken in the school:

The scoring is:
5 = strongly agree, 4 = agree, 3 = don't know, 2 = disagree,
1 = strongly disagree

How would your school score?

In my school: **Score:**
- Teachers give pupils the confidence to learn
- Pupils play an active part in the life of the school
- Good pastoral support is provided for pupils
- There is a relaxed but purposeful working atmosphere
- Staff and pupils feel safe and secure
- Most pupils feel a sense of achievement
- Teachers have high expectations of pupil behaviour
- Teachers have high expectations of pupil achievement
- The buildings and grounds are well maintained (p. 9)

BOLAM, R., McMAHON, A., POCKLINGTON, K. and WEINDLING, R. (1993) *Effective Management in Schools*, London: HMSO.

The linkage between the question about the purpose of schooling and the questions about the ethos of schools is that the articulated purpose of the school affects the way pupils are actually treated.

The clarity of the school purpose and the care taken with the ethos of the school are both important ethical indicators to the young people who spend so much time there. School models society, for children, and has a powerful influence on them and on the choices they make about how they live their lives. School teaches more than the basic skills and the formal syllabuses, and those schools where the staff understand their effect on the pupils, pay attention to every detail of their interactions.

How Are Organizational Structures Connected to the Purpose of the School?

Schools are basically organized in order to give pupils access to the quality of learning and teaching that those who work in the school believe is the best they can offer. Some educationalists use words such as *empowering* and *enabling* in order to describe the developmental nature of schools where the teachers are encouraged to be as much a part of the learning process as the pupils are: both staff and pupils are engaged in learning and teaching. David Hargreaves and David Hopkins (1991) link school culture, development planning and managing the school:

Through a review and revision of its management arrangements a school begins to transform its culture to support effective development planning. At the same time, the process of development planning will itself generate changes to the management arrangements and to the culture of the school. (p. 26)

Hargreaves and Hopkins see development planning as a systematic approach to the management of change. So what about schools that are not overtly in the middle of a change process, but are concerned with managing general daily learning and teaching? Starratt (1996) reminds his readers that:

The organization of the work of education should derive from the activities of learning and teaching. The work of educational administrators is to create, develop, support and encourage those organizational arrangements that flow organically from the core activities of the teaching and learning enterprise. (p. 5)

In other words, learning and teaching are the main 'business' of the school, and the school is organized in such a way as to prioritize these two activities. It is important that the management structure of the school supports the learning and teaching, and keeps them in view as its end-product. If the pupils and their learning needs are suppressed or diverted by the management structure, then the school cannot be effective.

In most schools in the UK, management structures include both middle and senior managers. Middle managers usually have responsibility for specific or multiple subject or pastoral areas, and senior managers have a whole-school responsibility. There are fewer senior managers than middle managers, but they officially have more power in the institution. Rosemary Webb (1994) in her final report on some research for the Association of Teachers and Lecturers wrote about the changing roles and responsibilities in primary schools in the UK since the Education Reform Act of 1988:

- greater delegation to, and reliance on, co-ordinators by headteachers;
- an increase in staff working co-operatively on curriculum planning and policy-making;
- the clarification of co-ordinator roles;
- the developing confidence and competence of co-ordinators themselves;
- opportunities to organize and/or provide INSET for colleagues. (p. vi)

Her research thus revealed a greater reliance on middle managers by senior management, and a more collaborative culture generally in primary schools. Indeed, before 1988, there were very few curriculum co-ordinators in primary schools, so it may be said that a whole new tier of management developed in primary education within the six years between the Education Reform Act, and the publication of Rosemary Webb's research.

Bolam et al. (1993) found explanations within different management structures about why there were differences in the responses to their research questions between primary and secondary schools:

Primary schools have relatively small and simple structures which are probably relatively easy to co-ordinate, whereas secondary schools are relatively large, complex and less easy to co-ordinate at school level, but probably more tightly structured and easier to co-ordinate at departmental level. It may well be the case, therefore, that primary headteachers and teachers are more likely to have a shared understanding of the various aspects of school management than their secondary colleagues, whereas the latter are more likely to have that shared understanding at departmental level. There was some evidence that **subject departments** were the key management structures in secondary schools but there was little evidence of inter-departmental collaboration. (pp. 124–125)

Who Informs the Management Decisions in a School?

Starratt (1996) — quoted in the last section — is an American writer. He uses the word *administrators* because in many of the states of the United States of America, educational administration is undertaken by a group of people who have a different career pattern and a different set of qualifications from many school leaders in this country and in Europe. In some states, after a minimum of about four years, teachers can follow a course of further study which allows them to become educational administrators. To a certain extent, they relinquish the overall responsibility for instructional leadership and become mainly responsible for the management of the physical space of the school, for the work of the teachers and for the attendance of the students. This may be a gross exaggeration and oversimplification, but it serves to point up the differences between 'management' and 'administration' which are explored further in Chapter 3.

Since the devolution of more power and responsibility to schools (and away from local authorities), some managers in education in this country find themselves spending too much time on administrative tasks and too little on the business of facilitating the learning and teaching in their schools. It is interesting to look at the formal organization of different schools — to trace who brings what experience to management teams — to see shifts in the recognition of important expertise. For example, a number of state schools employ bursars who do not necessarily have a background of teaching experience. They do have knowledge and experience of financial matters that are necessary for the local management of schools, and they are often members of the senior management team where they have a voice about education matters. This means that their financial advice influences management decisions about educational matters.

These questions may seem to imply that decisions about the learning and teaching in a school are made only by the members of the staff who have a place in management teams. In fact, legal responsibility for the business of a school lies with the governors, who usually do not have a professional background in education — Chapter 8 addresses these responsibilities in more detail. And the local community, including parents, employers and the pupils themselves all have a stake in the school,

> **Activity**
> **Think about the management teams in your school:**
>
> - What previous professional experience and values do members of the teams bring to the decisions about the learning and teaching in the school?
>
> - What experience, knowledge, values and qualities are *relevant* to inform decisions about learning and teaching?

and will wish to inform management decisions in some way. How they do so will be closely linked with the headteacher's values and the purpose of the school.

How Are Management Decisions Made in a School?

Many schools attempt transparency in their management systems by publishing plans or diagrams in school handbooks and in communications with parents, in order to show the formal management structures. This is an attempt to show official decision-making routes: it is an explanation of who goes to whom and in which order to discuss problems and possibilities within the structure of the school. The structure is meant to address both ease and flow of communication within a school, and to allow for effective consultation processes. In writing about educational organizations, decision-making and communication are sometimes closely linked.

But this is only the case where the leaders of the school are committed to open decision-making and where they believe that all should take part in decision-making. Bolam et al. (1993) found:

> Whereas the majority of teachers do want to be consulted about matters of school policy which affect their working lives, they do not necessarily want to be consulted about every aspect of daily school organization and maintenance. (p. 59)

And there is a very careful balance to be found between giving too much information, asking for too much consultation from busy people, and making uninformed decisions without any consultation. Whichever balance is found is based on the management philosophy of the senior managers in a school, and is then made public and clear to all the stakeholders of a school. In theory this is an effective way to run the decision-making processes of a school.

In practice however, it seems that the formal management and decision-making structures very rarely work in the way they are intended to work. When members of staff who are middle and senior managers attempt to define the formal and the informal decision-making processes and unofficial power-bases of their schools, they often find intriguing connections and liaisons within the informal power balances which block or circumvent the formal decision-making processes. Some surprisingly influential members of the staff are formally quite powerless in that their roles in the structure of the school do not officially give them much of a voice. But informally, through friendships and through other liaisons, they hold a great deal of power within discussions, which eventually sway the opinion of the rest of the staff. They may hold this power through quick and articulate verbal contributions to discussions; through humour; through having been at the school and developing a history and a knowledge of how the school works; or through alliances and contacts with other, more formally powerful, members of staff. Ball (1987) writes:

> Gossip and rumour are powerful but fragile channels of communication. They are arts of subversion. Humour may be used in a similar way. It is one of the most effective presentational styles for debunking in any situation. (p. 221)

Hoyle (1986) introduces the idea of 'micropolitical' influence to describe these inter-relationships and transactions. He describes the importance of information within an organization, and writes:

How information is acquired, distributed, presented, doctored or withheld is micropolitical. Information may be a 'good' to be exchanged and therefore be an element in exchange theory. But information is also a means of non-negotiable control. It is a powerful weapon in the armoury of headteachers who have access to different kinds of information. (p. 142)

It might be helpful at this point to explore these issues further by using your own school as an example:

Activity

You and Your Organization

Without discussion with other members of the staff, draw a picture, or a plan, or a map, or a diagram of your organization. Make sure that you put yourself in it. In one colour, mark in the **official** decision-making processes. This means the way decisions are officially supposed to be made — the way the structure might appear in a handbook. Show the gender of the people in power.

Then, in another colour, mark in the **unofficial** decision-making processes.

Are you able to mark in the unofficial decision-making routes? A knowledge of them depends on:

- accessibility — whether people talk about their friendships, alliances and rivalries within the staffroom;

- empathy — is it easy to see when colleagues are supporting each other non-verbally, when they are nodding in agreement, or searching the heavens in exasperation each time another member of staff speaks;

- length of tenure — it is very difficult to uncover all the unofficial decision-making routes because they are so unstated, so private and sometimes, so clandestine. Generally, it takes up to a year for a sensitive new member of staff to become aware of most of the micropolitical relationships within a school.

Excessive micropolitical activity within a school may be indicative of blocked or ineffective decision-making routes. For example, there might be individual members of the management structure who do not fulfil their management roles, and in this case do not act as a conduit for information and opinion, so other colleagues work round them, approaching other members of staff in order to expedite or clarify matters. Or it may be that the structure cannot function as such a conduit because it is not intended to do so: the senior management team does not wish to gather opinion and does not wish to share information. Whatever the cause of the excessive micropolitical activity, those with management responsibilities within a school need to be aware when they are overactive and to make some basic decisions about whether to use or to ignore the unofficial structures.

This is an ethical question — when passing information and when canvassing opinion, is it necessary to do so through overt or covert channels? Is it more important to 'get the job done', or to involve those with clearly assigned positions in the structure of the school in the process? 'Clearly assigned positions in the structure of the school' usually means that members of staff have undergone a formal recruitment procedure to achieve that position. In most schools, recruitment procedures are informed by equal opportunities guidelines which ensure a fairness and a transparency. In power groups that are formed by micropolitical activity, there is no such fairness and transparency. For example, in many schools in the UK, several members of staff celebrate the end of the week together in the pub on Friday evenings. Inevitably, friendship and influence groups form there, and staff members who have time to talk together in the pub and who find that they share values and opinions offer each other support when difficult issues are argued through in school. Indeed, arguments may be rehearsed and strategies planned in the pub.

Challenges to the influence of these support groups are often met with the response that the invitation is open to anyone to join the group — anyone can come to the pub after school on Fridays. But: those who have childcare responsibilities are not free to join; those who have asthma or breathing difficulties cannot usually sustain the smoky atmosphere of a pub, and there are several religious and ethnic groups that do not encourage the use of alcohol. In other words, these spontaneous support groups are *not* accessible and open to all. However, a well-managed school will ensure that where relevant, everybody on the staff, and young people and the local community and other stakeholders, will be canvassed in order to inform democratic decision-making.

Conclusion

Management structures and strategies can take over the business of a school, and disguise the real activities of learning and teaching. Managers who keep in mind their own philosophy of management, and their school's shared and clearly articulated direction will not be deflected from their targets. The culture and the organizational structures of an ethically managed school will be obvious to all those who work there, and will contribute to the overall development of the learning school.

References

BALL, S. (1987) *The Micro-politics of the School*, London: Routledge.

BARTH, R. (1990) *Improving Schools from Within; Teachers, Parents and Principals Can Make the Difference*, San Francisco: Jossey Bass.

BOLAM, R., MCMAHON, A., POCKLINGTON, K. and WEINDLING, R. (1993) *Effective Management in Schools*, London: HMSO.

DALIN, P. (1993) *Changing the School Culture*, London: Cassell.

HARGREAVES, D. and HOPKINS, D. (1991) *The Empowered School: The Management and Practice of Development Planning*, London: Cassell.

HOYLE, E. (1986) *The Politics of School Management*, London: Hodder and Stoughton.

MORTIMORE, P., SAMMONS, P., STOLL, L., LEWIS, D. and ECOB, R. (1989) *School Matters*, Wells: Open Books.

SENGE, P. (1990) *The Fifth Discipline*, London: Random House.

STARRATT, R. (1996) *Transforming Educational Administration*, New York: McGraw-Hill.

TAYLOR, P. (1993) *The Texts of Paulo Freire*, Buckingham: Open University Press.

WEBB, R. (1994) *After the Deluge: Changing Roles and Responsibilities in the Primary School*, London: Association of Teachers and Lecturers.

Chapter 3

Management and Leadership Styles

Key issues for managers:

- Who is a manager in education?

- Is it necessary to define differences between 'leadership' and 'management' and if so, what might they be?

- What different ways are there of describing leadership and management styles? Is it possible for a manager to make choices about which management style to employ?

- What can be imported constructively into education from Total Quality Management?

- Is educative leadership a particular management style?

- How might building and managing teams be connected with leadership values?

Who Is a Manager in Education?

It is sometimes said that *all* teachers are managers, and even the most inexperienced teacher is responsible for managing students' learning and behaviour in the classroom, and for managing their own work to meet students' needs. There may be some parallels between classroom management and school management, but there are also striking differences. For the purposes of this book, a manager in education is taken to be any member of staff who has responsibility for the work of other members of staff in order to ensure effective learning and teaching in the school.

> **Activity**
> List the members of staff in your school:
>
> Which of these members of staff do you manage, and which of them have management responsibility for you?
>
> What do you consider to be the main tasks in being a manager?
>
> What are the similarities and differences between managing adult members of staff and managing the learning of young people in the classroom?

Leadership or Management?

Many writers about leadership and management use the two terms interchangeably, and indeed in some circumstances, the terms 'managerialism' and 'administration' are also added without a careful differentiation between their meanings. Oldroyd, Elsner and Poster (1996) offer the following definitions in their international dictionary of educational management which clarify the differences:

> *leadership*: the process of guiding followers in a certain direction in pursuit of a vision, mission or goals; making and implementing and evaluating policy.

> *leader*: a person who exercises power, authority and influence over a group derived both from his or her acceptance by the group, and his or her position in the formal organization.

> *management*: a. the structure for and process of planning, co-ordinating and directing the activities of people, departments and organizations; getting things done with and through other people.
>
> b. the individual or group of individuals who manage an organization.

> *manager*: an individual responsible for the planning, co-ordination and direction of people, a department, or an organization.

> *managerialism*: the assumption that management is the solution to many organizational problems; often a pejorative term directed at those who see management as an end rather than a means, particularly in the publicly funded services.

> *administration*: the processes required to support the implementation of policies in organizations.

Within these definitions, it seems that management and leadership overlap to a certain extent, but leadership has an almost spiritual dimension, paying more attention to beliefs and values. Leaders also seem to have and to need a deeper understanding of power positions.

Everard and Morris (1996) see 'management' as a role and 'leadership' as the personal interaction that supports that role:

> Before we can set about our managerial role and mission, we need some skill in relating to other people. We need to understand the various behavioural processes which may be at work, and use our knowledge to influence or 'lead' individuals or groups. (p. 13)

The following exercise may help to clarify this discussion by applying it to 'real' people.

Activity

Set up three columns under the following headings: Leaders, Managers, Administrators. Now list all those people you work with at present and have worked with during your professional career, putting them under the relevant column heading. Then answer the following questions:

Was it easy to assign them to specific columns?

To what extent do the leaders and managers overlap?

Does this exercise show why 'leadership' and 'management' are so often used interchangeably?

Ways of Describing Styles of Leading and Managing

It is important to know about and be able to employ a selection of management and leadership styles because there are different ways of managing, several of which may be differently successful, depending on the ethos of the organization, the values of the manager, and what and who are to be managed. It is necessary to think about leadership and management styles not just to see how to motivate other teachers, but because it is reasonable to suppose that autocratic headteachers encourage a teacher-centred approach to learning and teaching in the classrooms over which they have responsibility, and democratic school leaders encourage more democracy and consultation all through their school so that learning and teaching is more likely to be student-centred.

In Chapter 1, we introduced a simple continuum of management styles and invited the reader to place themselves on it and then to answer some questions about how that choice was made. This continuum is based on writing and research about management from the 1950s by Tannenbaum and Schmidt, suggesting that managers who were more concerned with results were autocratic or paternalistic and told or persuaded those they managed to do what was necessary. Those managers who were more concerned with good relationships with those they managed were more likely to be consultative or democratic. Thus a binary was set up where it was expected that managers could be either people or task oriented, but rarely both. In some ways, although this division is a simplistic and incomplete one, there are still managers in schools today who rely on systems, strategies and paperwork, and do not pay enough attention to the needs and attributes of the people with whom they work. There are other managers who are so focused on people and on keeping everyone happy that they do not achieve the task, much to the frustration of those they manage. It could also be seen that some of the quality management literature (described later in this chapter) imported unexamined into education management in the 1990s might lead managers back to too much emphasis on tasks and systems.

In the 1960s, the models for describing management styles became more multi-dimensional, and writers such as Blake and Mouton published a questionnaire from which a position on a grid was extrapolated. The grid showed whether the manager was high or low in concern for people or relationships, and also introduced attributes in the manager such as assertiveness, solicitude, gaining commitment, being good at administration, or passively exerting minimum effort. This work seems highly judgmental now, and seemed to suggest that there was only one correct way to manage — in the scoring system of the questionnaire, top marks went to the motivational manager who gained commitment from the workers.

Mainstream literature about education management published since the 1950s until the early 1980s appeared to take no account of gender, but in the middle to late 1980s, there was a proliferation of management literature based on research which looked at the contrasts in the ways that men and women managed organizations. Writers such as Judi Marshall (1984) wrote that those leaders who fitted a *feminine leadership model* were more likely to operate co-operatively, were happier working with a team structure, were committed to quality output, were intuitive as well as rational problem solvers, and had key characteristics of lower control, empathy, and were collaborative. Those who fitted a *masculine leadership model* operated competitively, worked better within or leading a hierarchy, were committed to winning, were rational problem-solvers, and had key characteristics of high control, unemotional strategy planning, and were analytical in their approach.

In general, at this time and in the literature, women's management styles were characterized as more responsive to issues of morality, ethics and principle, because they were concerned with involving those they managed in procedures such as decision-making processes, but women did not come out of this literature with particularly effective or professional reputations. This was because the profiles into which they were fitted often made it seem as though they could not make decisions without reference to many other people, which was seen as too reactive and time-consuming; and they could not be assertive because they were too busy being understanding and supportive. In a sense, women were seen as too 'soft' and ineffective to manage large organizations. And the skills and attributes seen as important were connected with organizational efficiency and technical excellence — the skills necessary to do timetables and to develop management systems, and to win were reified.

Ten years later, it is clear that these profiles were often too rigid, and also seemed to encompass all women, making no allowance for any notion that some men manage sensitively, and some women manage in a dominating and authoritarian fashion. They also placed women in a deficit model by taking for granted that the management skills that many of them appeared to have developed would not fit them to manage the education systems in which they worked.

Writing about management styles published in the mid-1990s seems to be far more realistic and helpful to others working in the field because it introduces new descriptors for all managers. Bolam, McMahon, Pocklington and Weindling (1993) wrote up a fascinating piece of research, which, when set in the context of education management in the UK, shows the tensions between the way teachers would like to be managed, and the market place ideology in which education management takes place. They found that:

> the principle features and processes associated with the effective management of their schools, as perceived by the teachers and headteachers in the sample [included that]:

> *The headteacher and the senior management team*

> - Work well together as a team; have roles and responsibilities which are clear to staff; are highly visible and approachable.

- Take the key decisions but consult staff before doing so; face up to differences of opinion and work for a negotiated solution and a sense of joint ownership of school developments.

- Model desired behaviours and attributes (e.g. hard work, commitment, mutual support and teamwork); behave with honesty and integrity in straightforward and non-devious ways; behave as if accountable to staff by providing clear evidence of the outcomes of their action; are ready to admit mistakes and consider alternatives.

- Are good at 'people' management, including identifying and mobilizing individual talents; regularly brief teachers about day-to-day issues; delegate meaningful tasks in order to develop and empower staff; monitor delegated tasks.

- Convey to staff a sense that the school is under control; support teachers' work in the classroom; provide good and consistent support to the staff; promote the school's image in the community. (p. 120)

Activity

Note the ways in which management styles are described in this quotation.

Can you fit them into either the masculine or feminine leadership models described earlier on p. 27 based on the work of Judi Marshall?

Valerie Hall published *Dancing on the Ceiling* in 1996, in which she studies women managers in education. She writes that the intention of her book 'is not to prove that . . . similarities are the consequences of gender, but to show how gender has an impact on leadership behaviour in the context of education, by focusing on women's experiences' (p. 16). So, her findings are important for all managers in education. She finds ways of describing managing education organizations that allow women to enter the discourses of management in the late 1990s while clearly retaining their values. The quote from *Dancing on the Ceiling* on pages 11 and 12 seems to describe women headteachers who can do both.

It may be helpful to take the descriptive words out of the quotations from Bolam et al. and Hall, and to see whether they build into a classic manager or a leader, and whether these descriptors — both sets of which are derived from research among teachers — are possible ways of managing in schools in the UK in the late twentieth century within the market place ideology that surrounds schooling.

The Quality Management Movement

Most of the theories about leadership and management described previously derive from general management literature — only the more recent research was based within education. The Quality Movement, characterized by Total Quality Management (TQM), was originally adopted by organizations nationally and internationally at the end of the 1980s. It is an approach to management based on the works of Crosby (1979) and Deming (1986). It was adopted by and imported into literature about school management very influentially in the late 1980s and early 1990s.

Davies, Ellison, Osborne and West-Burnham (1990) describe TQM in the following way:

> The principles were first applied in Japanese industry but are now finding increasing acceptance in the UK. The essence of TQM is the process of reducing costs by improving quality, so enhancing customer satisfaction. A crucial contribution of TQM theory is the redefinition of the concept of the customer. Although, traditionally, customers are perceived as external to the organization, TQM defines *all working relationships* in terms of customer satisfaction and quality is defined in terms of conformity to customer requirements. (pp. 68–69)

All working relationships (our emphasis) mean that relationships in schools are redefined as customer/consumer. In this way everyone in a school is a customer of someone else. Pupils and parents are repositioned by quality management theorists into having a more central and a louder voice in decisions about the school and its activities. Other stakeholders, too, are seen as part of the decision-making process, and are made more powerful in relation to the school by quality management. Better communication is encouraged within and into the organization, so that the customer's views can be canvassed; teams and teamwork are seen as significant to the organization; the organization and its structure are carefully defined; change is managed with great reliance on evaluation and monitoring procedures; and there is a commitment to continuous improvement through development.

There are problems with this work in relation to education. Gewirtz, Ball and Bowe (1995) argue that some of the literature on quality management in schools encourages school leaders to pay too much attention to the technical aspects of management without taking into account the political and social contexts of education. They also maintain that the texts which introduce quality management issues to schools use collaborative management styles instrumentally, so that conflict is managed in such a way as to disappear and those who are managed are expected to be made to agree with those who do the managing. Conflict resolution goes into quietening dissent rather than taking note of it. A similar point is made by Fullan and Hargreaves (1992) when they write about 'contrived collegiality' as a way of controlling teachers through meetings and teamwork. Such control may operate through:

> curriculum coordinators, mentor schemes, joint planning in specifically provided rooms, school-based management, formally scheduled meetings and clear job descriptions and training programmes for those in consultative roles. (p. 78)

The basic principles of quality management are the basic principles of all good management, but they need an ethical and values-based framework which is clearly tuned to educational needs.

Quality Control and Quality Assurance

These terms are often used interchangeably, or as West-Burnham (1992) writes, there is an 'uncertain and often ambiguous use of the terms inspection, quality control, quality assurance and quality management' (p. 15). He goes on to show that *Quality control* is concerned with product testing, and the responsibility for it lies with supervisors. It includes limited quality criteria and some self-inspection, and most of the systems used are paper-based. *Quality assurance* uses statistical process control, emphasizes prevention, makes use of external accreditation, delegates involvement, includes the audit of quality systems, and includes cause and effect analyses.

Fidler (1996) explains the difference between quality control and quality assurance as:

> The customary process of ensuring a quality output is quality control. This involves inspecting the output of a process and rejecting anything that fails to achieve the required level of quality. School self-evaluation is a form of Quality Control. It takes place *after the event*. The alternative form of ensuring quality is Quality Assurance. This involves designing systems to deliver quality *before the event*. The professional training of teachers is one aspect of a quality assurance process. (p. 37)

At the centre of this definitional difficulty is the conflict and tension between accountability and improvement. Writers about education try to fit inspection into the quality categories above. It depends on whether inspection is seen as a means of accountability or of helping schools to improve. For accountability purposes inspection might be seen as quality control, and for school improvement purposes, it may be seen as quality assurance.

Competency-based Leadership and Management

In the UK there has been a considerable thrust to develop competency-based standards for those at all levels in schools from newly qualified teachers to those aspiring for headship. The move to competency-based assessment (for example, to assessing performance rather than knowledge) is part of a national commitment to developing competence-based qualifications across all occupations. The Management Charter Initiative has already developed generic standards for managers, and these were translated for use in education. The recently introduced National Professional Qualification for Headship attempts to relate a set of skills and attributes to what the TTA define as 'the key areas of headship': strategic direction and development of the school, teaching and learning, leading and managing staff, efficient and effective deployment of staff and resources, and accountability. The necessary skills and attributes are listed under the following headings:

- leadership skills, attributes and professional competence: the ability to lead and manage people to work as individuals and as a team towards a common goal;

- decision-making skills: the ability to investigate, solve problems and make decisions;

- communication skills: the ability to make points clearly and understand the views of others;

- self-management: the ability to plan time effectively and to organize oneself well. (TTA, 1997)

Esp (1993, p. 15) raises a series of questions about the limits to competence-based assessments for schools managers that are pertinent to the evaluation of the National Professional Qualification for Headship. Among these are the following concerns:

How can one assess that candidates can undertake many competences at once, rather than sequentially?

How can one assess good judgment?

How can one assess moral leadership?

There are many right ways to manage, how can these be assessed reliably?

> **Activity**
> Is the competence-based approach able to encompass the conception of the educational leader as a leader of culture and values?
>
> Or is it only able to work on management skills, rather than those higher level qualities of leadership?

Being competent is not the same thing as having competences, how can one develop the whole person?

Esp's (1993, p. 15) final question is directly relevant to the National Qualification: how can one assess team competence? In schools the headteacher does not have to do everything herself, collective competence is the important issue.

Educative Leadership

Management must be educative for both those who manage and those who are managed. Duignan and Macpherson (1992) write:

> Educative leadership is far more than a set of social or management techniques evident in the skills or style of an individual, such as a school principal, or in the behaviours of a group comprising the executive team of an institution or a system. It is more concerned with ways of knowing, valuing and altering the organization.
>
> Educative leadership inevitably questions the arbitrary exercise of social power. We find it very difficult to assume that wisdom about education is hierarchically distributed in an organization or that a bureaucratic rationality about structures and functions is self-justified. We hold that the responsible use of social power in education is an essential feature of educative leadership. (p. 4)

So educative leadership is not a management or leadership style — it is more a desired outcome of management and leadership which encompasses all the relationships, and the learning and teaching in a school. A school which benefits from educative leadership has an ethos of energy and respect for all the stakeholders involved, and it is committed to a constant examination of the ethical bases of decisions made.

Teambuilding and Working with a Team

An introduction to thinking about teams and teambuilding is included within this chapter because an educative leader is committed to working constructively with teams of people rather than just individuals for many different reasons, among them:

- they are part of a democratic and consultative way of working;
- they share the load;
- they go further than one person alone could;
- they are a marvellous arena for professional development;
- they allow two-way communication so that managers are able to hear what those who are managed have to say;
- when they are well-managed, team meetings are exciting, creative and stimulating.

It is taken for granted now that the planning, delivery and monitoring of the curriculum in schools is organized through teams of teachers. Curriculum team leadership is usually seen as a middle management activity, and leadership of whole-school task teams is seen as senior management activity. Teachers in schools find themselves in many different teams, leading some and having junior membership of others. Each team seems to build its own customs and rules very quickly, and depending on how it is chaired, team members find it easier or more difficult to find their voices in some teams and not in others.

Activity
List all the teams that you take part in or manage during a school year.

1 Try to present them all as a Venn diagram with linked circles. The linkage could be when the same people are involved in different teams, or when you are a member of one team through your membership of another team, or when the teams' tasks are linked.
2 Colour them differently to signify your official power position in each one — which do you lead, which do you co-lead, which are you a junior member of?
3 Think about your unofficial power positions in each team — in which do you feel creative, which do you feel at ease in? Do you look forward to attending the meetings of this team, and do you feel energized by the meetings? Which teams do you feel silenced in? Do any teams seem to be holding a conversation above your head or one that began when you were not present?
4 Is there a connection between the ways the teams are led or chaired, and the way you and others value your attendance at these team meetings?

Team Roles

Teams of people are often more productive than one person alone because teams are made up of people with different ways of thinking and acting. These differences can make for creative energy that is enabling and exciting, but if the differences are not managed well, they can become disabling and stressful for those in the team. Meredith Belbin (1993) found that there are some important roles that are essential to the creativity and productivity of a team. He lists nine sets of personality traits of team members, and maintains that although not every team should have nine members, a team works best when the following roles have attention paid to them (but several can be played by one team member):

Plant
Advances new ideas and strategies with special attention to major issues and looks for possible breaks in approach to the problems with which the group is confronted. Is creative, imaginative, and unorthodox.

Resource Investigator
Explores and reports on ideas, developments and resources outside the group; creates external contacts that may be useful to the team and conducts any subsequent negotiations. Is extrovert, enthusiastic and communicative.

Chair
Controls the way in which a team moves towards the group objectives by making the best use of team resources; recognizes where the team's strengths and weaknesses lie; and ensures that the best use is made of each team member's potential. Is mature and confident, and clarifies goals while promoting decision-making and delegating well.

Shaper
Shapes the way in which team effort is applied; directs attention generally to the setting of objectives and priorities; and seeks to impose some shape or pattern on group discussion and on the outcome of group activities. Is challenging and dynamic, and thrives on pressure while having the drive and confidence to overcome obstacles.

Monitor-Evaluator
Analyses problems and evaluates ideas and suggestions so that the team is better placed to take balanced decisions. Is sober, strategic and discerning, and judges situations accurately.

Team Worker
Supports members in their strengths (e.g. building on suggestions); underpins members in their shortcomings; improves communications between members and fosters team spirit generally. Is co-operative, mild, perceptive and diplomatic. Listens, builds, averts friction and calms.

Implementer
Turns concepts and plans into practical working procedures; carries out agreed plans systematically and efficiently. Is disciplined, reliable and conservative.

Completer
Ensures that the team is protected as far as possible from mistakes of both commission and omission; actively searches for aspects of work which need a more than usual degree of attention; and maintains a sense of urgency within the team. Is painstaking, conscientious and anxious.

Specialist
Is single-minded, self-starting and dedicated. Provides knowledge and skills in rare supply.

An effective team leader will be particularly aware of these necessarily different ways of operating, because they can cause friction. For example, the drive and originality of the shaper can irritate and be irritated by the painstaking orderliness of the completer. Or the sober prudence of the monitor-evaluator may well exasperate the unorthodox and individualistic plant. A major part of a team leader's responsibility to the team will be to make sure that they all work together.

Clearly the implications of Belbin's work for a manager or leader are that an awareness of these necessary characteristics ensures both that teams are built up around differences, and that the differences are celebrated and welcomed. When a team appears not to function as well as it could, it might be helpful to think about the roles listed above and to recognize gaps or dissonances. The person responsible for the team will then either find someone to fill the gap, or will encourage the team to develop new ways of working together to make up for the missing way of working. Or the leader will encourage the warring members to value the differences and to see how necessary they are for the productivity of the team.

Team leaders may also need to be reminded from time to time that teams are not static. Classically, teams (and classes) in schools go through stages in working together which have strong emotional dynamics:

forming — usually a calm and brief stage where members are formal and polite, investing little emotionally in the processes of the team, but quietly trying to work out the rules;

storming — this is usually the most uncomfortable time for team members and team leaders: conflicts and sub-groups emerge and the authority of the leader is questioned. Basic values and the task itself are challenged. This is a very emotional stage which often seems unproductive but exhausting;

norming — after the high emotional energy of the storming stage, the team usually settles down to work together, reconciling, celebrating and valuing differences, and cooperating to achieve the task;

performing — this is often the most satisfying stage when people really work as a team, supporting each other, communicating in a common 'language' and working flexibly and productively together.

One might add to these four:

adjourning — teams in education may end as soon as they reach the performing stage because of the nature of the academic year. The temptation of the team leader is to ignore imminent endings in order to maintain the performing stage as long as possible, because there is rarely enough time to finish properly;

mourning — in education organizations particularly, the academic year means that many teams begin and end during the year, so attention must be paid to the emotional 'fall out' that endings bring. Team members who have not been given time to mourn their previous incarnations as a team will find it more difficult to commit themselves to the new team.

Conclusion

This chapter has described writing and thinking about management and leadership styles. An understanding of these issues is important for managers in education so that they can make more conscious and informed choices about the way they lead or manage. As we wrote in Chapter 1, ways of leading and managing depend on values and ethos, and on what and who are to be managed. This introduction to a range of possible styles allows for a wider set of options and a portfolio of different styles to be employed in different circumstances.

References

BELBIN, M. (1993) *Team Roles at Work*, Oxford: Butterworth-Heinemann.

BLAKE, R.R. and MOUTON, J.S. (1964) *The Managerial Grid*, Houston, TX: Gulf Publishing.

BOLAM, R., MACMAHON, A., POCKLINGTON, K. and WEINDLING, D. (1993) *Effective Management in Schools*, London: HMSO.

CROSBY, P.B. (1979) *Quality is Free*, New York: McGraw-Hill.

DAVIES, B., ELLISON, L., OSBORNE, A. and WEST-BURNHAM, J. (1990) *Education Management for the 1990s*, Harlow: Longman.

DEMING, W.E. (1986) *Out of the Crisis*, MIT Center for Advanced Engineering Study.

DUIGNAN, P.A. and MACPHERSON, R.J.S. (1992) *Educative Leadership*, London: Falmer Press.

ESP, D. (1993) *Competences for School Managers*, London: Kogan Page.

EVERARD, K. and MORRIS, G. (1996) *Effective School Management*, London: Paul Chapman Publishing.

FIDLER, B. (1996) *Strategic Planning for School Improvement*, London: Pitman Publishing.

FULLAN, M. and HARGREAVES, D. (1992) *What's Worth Fighting for in Your School*, Buckingham: Open University Press.

GEWIRTZ, S., BALL, S. and BOWE, R. (1995) *Markets, Choices and Equity in Education*, Buckingham: Open University.

HALL, V. (1996) *Dancing on the Ceiling*, London: Paul Chapman Publishing.

MARSHALL, J. (1984) *Women Managers: Travellers in a Male World*, Chichester: John Wiley & Sons.

OLDROYD, D., ELSNER, D. and POSTER, C. (1996) *Educational Management Today: A Concise Dictionary and Guide*, London: Paul Chapman Publishing.

TANNENBAUM, R. and SCHMIDT, W.H. (1973) 'How to choose a leadership pattern', *Harvard Business Review*, **36**, pp. 95–101.

TEACHER TRAINING AGENCY (1997) *National Standards for Headteachers*, London.

WEST-BURNHAM, J. (1992) *Managing Quality in Schools*, Harlow: Longman.

Chapter 4

Working with People, Part One — Management Skills

There is undoubtedly a key set of interpersonal skills for managers in schools. An examination of these skills helps answer the question: how does a manager work best with colleagues in order to ensure that the highest quality of learning and teaching takes place in their school? Schools and other organizations develop systems and strategies which take account of planning systems and strategic activities. But tasks are only productive if the people involved complete them willingly and with commitment and with some autonomy. Some of the most important skills for managers are those of self-management: these are well-developed in a good manager, who can then in turn help those with whom they manage to develop the skills. Other skills are directly concerned with the interpersonal: they are necessary when working with other people.

Key issues for managers:

- prioritizing;

- managing time;

- decision-making;

- strategic planning;

- managing conflict;

- working with difficult people;

- motivating;

- delegating;

- managing stress.

Section One: Self and Systems Management Skills

Skills of self- and systems management are linked to two underpinning principles:

- a clear articulation of the educational and management values of the manager;

- that those values help inform the manager about which management activities and decisions are important.

Prioritizing

Managers may be overwhelmed by the number of tasks they have to complete (often at the same time) and sometimes they can only hope to balance and move their duties around as a juggler might. The precarious nature of this juggling is so absorbing (and exciting when well done) that it is easy to get to the stage where another task is taken on almost automatically because a request for help has been made. In other words, the main management task becomes getting all the jobs and requests completed without mishap and without question. One of the problems with the proliferating bureaucracy in schools in the UK has been that teachers and managers have no time to reflect or to ask themselves *why* they are completing certain activities — they only know that they have to do so, and that completion is expected of them. The bureaucratization of teaching has been seen by some commentators, for example Ball, (1994) as a way of controlling teachers — it is not coincidental that the Education Reform Act of 1988 was introduced just after the prolonged teachers' action of the mid-1980s. It is hardly surprising therefore that reluctance or questioning by teachers may be interpreted as resistance, rather than a professional activity.

So, to return to the management tasks spinning around in the air, how might a manager decide which task to address first, or indeed whether to address them all? There are various management strategies which help prioritize, such as brainstorming everything, then making connections between items, and numbering them in a logical order. But what makes the order logical, and how are the connections clarified? Basically, education and management values help inform the varying weights of importance and levels of immediacy. So, an ability to step back from the juggling and to reflect on relative value and importance will inform the order of priority.

Managing time

Time management is rather like prioritizing in that it is not a simple value-free skill. It does depend on values — how do you and your organization value the different activities you spend your time on? A time log is a most educative process as a way of analysing the way time is spent:

Activity
Construct and complete a **time log** to be completed every half hour during one school day, under the headings:

- What happened?

- Time taken?

- People involved?

- Any comments?

Here are some suggestions to improve time usage, if a time log reveals any surprises:

1   Try to avoid crisis management by:

- always planning ahead. Keep action dates in your diary — the dates by which things need to be done — these should always be in advance of deadline dates — to allow for problems, panics or emergencies;

- always building in thinking time to any plans — whether for the week ahead or for long term projects. Try to avoid this time being eroded by routine jobs;

- occasionally analysing how you are spending your time. It is useful to do this sometimes by analysing a day, sometimes by looking back over a longer period.

2   Ensure that meetings are always necessary and effective — well-planned; with agendas; make brief action minutes; agree time limits on meetings and on agenda items. Be clear about the purpose of a meeting — is it information-giving or decision-making? Staff easily become disillusioned if it becomes obvious that a decision has really already been made. Always consider whether there is a better, less time-consuming way to deal with the subject of the meeting.

3   Dealing with the paper mound — a golden rule is: apart from sorting **only deal with each document once**. It is helpful to have a sorting system, for example:

- **DUMP**   superfluous and useless — get rid of it
- **DELAY**   important matters — needing time and thought, consciously file separately to be dealt with later
- **DELEGATE** are you the best/right person to deal with this? If not pass on
- **DO**   things (usually routine or statistical), which you have to do and can be done fairly easily. Either do immediately or decide when you will do them.

4   Keep one action list of things to do. Complete it at the same time each day and remember to carry forward things which are not completed today. Do not worry about not completing everything you put down for each day, but try to get increasingly realistic about what can be accomplished so that you can reduce the pressure on yourself. Number items in the order you think they will be done — but prioritize and asterisk the most important. Group items together, for example, do all telephone calls together.

5   Learn to say 'no'!

6   Avoid procrastination! Get something down on paper; plan to work for at least ten minutes (once started things often get going); sub-divide large tasks, make the rest manageable and so on.

7   Have a good filing system — know where to find things.

Decision-Making

Managers who make decisions quickly often regret their speed. It is helpful to take enough time and distance to be able to see the factors involved in decision-making clearly. This is another instance when the reflective manager is more effective. It may be helpful to answer the following questions before the decision-making process begins:

- who it is necessary to invite to inform the decision-making process?
- is the process itself to be educative and persuasive?
- how wide-reaching will the consequences of the decisions be?
- who will be affected by the decisions?
- who will be persuaded by the outcomes and who will need more persuasion?
- how important is it that the final decision holds?
- how important is it to the team that the process leading up to the decision is consultative and involves genuine discussion?

Some decisions are best taken by the manager alone, some need the input of the whole team, and some are to be informed by the team but ultimately taken by the team leader. Everard and Morris (1996, p. 40) suggest that logical steps towards decision-taking include: the definition of the situation, the establishment of relevant criteria, the generation of alternatives, evaluation and testing of suggestions, and finally the selection of a course of action.

Strategic Planning

Brian Fidler (1996) describes strategy in a way that shows how ideas of strategic planning in education have evolved, and have been taken over almost completely by notions of school development planning which involve the whole organization. In other words, 'strategic' has come to mean 'whole organization'.

> Strategy is concerned with the long-term future of an organisation — that which makes it distinctive, the broad direction it takes . . . it is the plan which integrates all the actions of the school. (p. 1)

Strategic planning is included in this section of this chapter because, in many ways, every educative activity works best when it is carefully planned for, regardless of the number of people involved. Bell (1992) writes 'the decision to plan any change can be seen as an attempt to impose direction and purpose on anticipated future events' (p. 150). Does careful planning give us more control over the future? And does institutional planning give us more control over the people working within the institution? Some managers see planning as problem-solving, and others see it as making sense of and planning for the future. A school must have the ability to deal with both contingencies: to find ways round existing and future problems and to make plans which put projected aims into reality.

Strategic planning — making aims real — is a management skill that ensures energy is not spent needlessly or aimlessly, and that outcomes are more focused on needs and less haphazard than they might have been. School development planning has become a very precise science and many writers, including Hargreaves and Hopkins (1994), have published very helpful guides to, and analysis of, effective institutional development planning.

There are several instruments which can be used for all or part of the planning process, and that appeal to different managers depending on what is to be decided, how it is to be planned for, and who is involved in the planning process. They also appeal to different ways of thinking — some are very meticulous and thorough, and others allow space for creativity and lack of clear definition. The instruments are often known as problem-solving instruments, and could be used by individuals or by whole organizations — some may work for you and some may not.

One planning strategy is summarized by the acronym TOSIPAR. It is really just a very logical and systematic way of thinking about a problem and planning an approach to solve it. The letters stand for:

Tuning in
Objective setting
Success criteria
Information and ideas gathering
Planning
Action
Review to improve

TOSIPAR is a very methodical approach to planning and problem solving, and helps clarify when stages in a process have been inadequately handled.

Figure 4.1: The Diagnostic Window

Open to change	**Open to change**
Working well	**Not working well**
Working well and open to change	Not working well and open to change
Working well and not open to change	Not working well and not open to change
Working well	**Not working well**

Not open to change   ***Not open to change***

The **Diagnostic Window** (see *Figure 4.1*) helps identify a problem area that can then be worked on more closely. If there is general awareness of a problem, but no apparent specific clarification about which area is most open to change, the diagnostic window is used by brainstorming the issues and classifying them into the different spaces below. It becomes clear that it probably is not necessary to address the issues that appear in 'working well and open to change'; and that the issues that end up in 'working well and not open to change' and 'not working well and not open to change' cannot be addressed — they are not open to change.

From this activity, it will become clear that energy is best spent on the quadrant labelled 'Not working well and open to change'.

Figure 4.2: SWOT analysis

Strengths	Weaknesses
Opportunities	Threats

Where would you like to be?
Use this model on your own institution: can you change weaknesses into strengths and threats into opportunities?

A **SWOT Analysis** (*Figure 4.2*) will help to decide what changes to make after the problem area has been identified:

This is a useful instrument for changing attitudes and seeing that areas perceived as threats and weaknesses may well be seen as opportunities and promises. Both the Diagnostic Window and the SWOT Analysis combine logic with creative thought. They are very helpful activities which can be used to clarify and plan problem-solving strategies when problems are unclear and seemingly insurmountable.

Figure 4.3: Force-field analysis

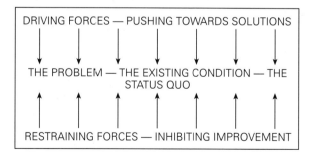

Source: Force-field Analysis (LEWIN, 1948)

Force-field Analysis as a planning and problem-solving tool. After defining the problem carefully, problem-solvers should brainstorm both the Driving Forces and the Restraining Forces and line them up opposite one another, with the original problem in between (see *Figure 4.3*). The task is to analyse the driving and restraining forces individually and very carefully. The problem-solver is to develop strategies for strengthening the Driving Forces and weakening the Restraining Forces so that the problem, the status quo, moves towards solution:

These skills depend on clarity of thought and an ability to transmit and encourage that clarity in others. They are quite easily learnt and used, but are most valuable when they are driven by a clear philosophy of management in education.

Section Two: Managing with Other People

Skills implicit in managing with other people are interpersonal skills — they depend on the personal values of the manager, and the way those values impact on the manager's relationships with other people.

Managing Conflict

Everard and Morris (1996) are clear that the ability to handle conflict is a key factor in what they call 'managerial' success:

> Whenever we wish to make changes, there is potential for conflict. Furthermore, we not only have to handle situations in which there is conflict between ourselves and one or more other members of staff but may also at times have to resolve conflicts between our subordinates or, most difficult of all, to plot a course through the minefield of 'politics' when two of our peers or superiors are locked in struggle. (p. 88)

In this description, conflict seems an inevitable part of managing in schools, and an understanding of the sources of it, an empathy for those who are overcome by it, and some strategies for dealing with it, must be part of all managers' set of interpersonal skills.

Many textbooks about management in education write about managing conflict as quite unproblematic:

> This chapter deals with the nature of conflict, how it builds up, its positive and negative effects and some guidelines for handling conflict situations. (Everard and Morris, 1996, p. 88)

They then make conflict management a safer activity by offering diagrams, continuums and questionnaires as theoretical explanations. Caldwell and Spinks (1988) include a chapter about the management of conflict, where they write:

> Collaborative School Management provides a framework for coping with the conflict that is inevitable when there are different views of the ends and means of education, and when people with different, often ambiguous areas of responsibility seek to achieve their purposes with limited resources. (p. 200)

But such books seem to miss out the enormously strong feelings aroused by commonly shared experiences and understanding of conflict. Many people, particularly women, say that their fear of conflict is one of the reasons that stops them from planning to become managers. They worry that they will not deal well with conflict, and that they and others involved will be hurt by it. This is probably because in our society, conflict is thought to be closely allied to violence. Kenway and Fitzclarence (1997) write:

> the definition of violence has widened. It is increasingly understood that violence occurs along a continuum and involves physical, sexual, verbal and emotional abuses of power at individual, group and social structural levels. (p. 117)

So, misuse and abuse of power are seen as forms of violence, and can often feel as oppressive and painful as physical violence to those involved in them as well as to those who witness them, and the fear that threatens many people is that the outcomes of conflict are often presented as verbal abuses of power. This common merging of conflict with violence is not helpful to managers because while the effects of violence naturally arouse fear, if that fear then accrues around all ideas of conflict, fear can paralyse most attempts to deal with conflict.

One way of separating conflict from violence (of seeing violence as only one of many responses to conflict) is to think more carefully about the whole concept of conflict. It might be helpful to remember that all drama — plays, theatre, radio, television and film — are based on conflict and its resolution. It can be no coincidence that teachers who have a background in teaching drama are among those who think most productively about conflict when management courses address working with and managing conflict.

This brainstorm will almost certainly begin with negative, strong and uncomfortable words, describing the feelings nearest the surface that make it more difficult for managers to be nonchalant and calm about managing conflict. But eventually, the positive aspects come:

> **Activity**
> **Thinking about conflict**
> 1   Brainstorm the word 'conflict', preferably in a black pen.
> 2   Colour code the brainstorm, using red for positive words and blue for negative words. Some words will be both positive and negative.

> Conflict is not necessarily a negative force; it can be an opportunity for both growth and mutual support among professionals who most often work in isolation. (Blase and Blase, 1994, p. 25)

Usually, recognition follows that well-managed conflict can be productive and creative, and can move a group of people or an organization on to a far more productive phase than the one it was 'stuck' in before.

The next part of this chapter looks at a particular aspect of managing conflict — working with difficult people.

Working with Difficult People

It is important when thinking about difficult people to think not just about anger and negativity, but also about those who need to be moved forward. There are some members of staff who might be quite at ease where they are in the school and working as they do, but it is clear to those who work with them that their professional development has ceased. Some of these concerns are explored further in Chapter 5.

However, here is one strategy for working carefully through some of the issues contained within working with difficult people. It is usually best done in groups of three people who have agreed about listening carefully to each other, who are paying careful attention to confidentiality, who understand that it is necessary to take turns to look carefully at uncomfortable feelings, and who have explored how best to give constructive feedback.

If, however, you have no other 'safe' people with whom to do this exercise, try putting yourself in the place of your difficult person, but only for a short while! The suggestions for reflection after the activity may help you move forward in your dealings with this person.

Activity

Working with Difficult People

A By yourself, write about someone inside or outside your organization with whom you find it difficult to work.   ***15 minutes***

B Work in groups of three, preferably people you have not worked with before. One of the group takes ***10 minutes*** to describe the personality and the situation to be explored — they set the scene.

C The person offering the description rôle plays the person described, and one of the other two rôle plays the person trying to resolve the situation. The third member of the group acts as observer and keeps time. ***10 minutes***

D Spend ***10 minutes*** giving feedback and discussing the rôle play. The observer leads the feedback, but all three members of the group should take part in the discussion.

Repeat the whole exercise three times, so that everyone has experienced all three rôles.

Timekeeping is very important — no matter how absorbing the problem is, try to keep to the times given.

After completing this activity, some of the conclusions drawn about working with difficult people might well include the following suggestions from Gold (1998):

- Acknowledging the uncomfortable feelings aroused in you by your difficult person, then trying to put them aside to work objectively with the problem.

- Separating the person from the problem — try to focus more on your shared present difficulty, rather than on your shared history of misunderstanding or animosity.

- Taking time — trying not to react immediately, and therefore making sure that you are not in your usual unproductive pattern with this person. Make time to think quietly about your next action, so that it is proactive rather than reactive.

- Developing a network of people whose values you share and who are in the same sort of position as you, so that you can support each other with each person's difficult people.

- Planning your actions carefully — if you do not have the opportunity to discuss your problem, at least rehearse the next conversation for yourself — traffic jams and showers are ideal places for loud but private monologues!

Motivation

Managers often think about motivation in relation to other people — to those they manage — but do not link these thoughts with what motivates themselves (although they are quite clear about this). Good teaching and learning is based on theories of motivation, so teachers, whether consciously or subconsciously, think about how to work constructively with other people all through their professional careers. Inevitably, teachers are expert both in what motivates them and in what motivates others. Skilled managers transfer this expertise to managing with other professionals quite easily.

Before exploring theories of motivation more carefully there are some warnings to note. Motivation without clear underpinning values can easily become manipulation: persuading people to do what the institution apparently needs without balancing the needs of the individual with the needs of the organization, or without paying attention to the agreed aims of the school, may result in a dysfunctional organization. Teachers, who work at a high level of thought and analysis about their own activities, are quick and perceptive when they themselves are managed without thought and analysis. They become cynical and resistant to persuasion if they suspect that they are being manipulated.

Everard and Morris (1996) write;

'Motivation' can be defined as 'getting results through people' or 'getting the best out of people'. The second definition is slightly preferable, since 'the best' which people can offer is not necessarily synonymous with 'the results' which we might initially want from them, though it should be in line with the overall goals and ethos of the school. (p. 20)

They go on to describe two theories of motivation:

- Maslow's (1943) hierarchy of needs, which sets human needs at different levels within a hierarchy, through which we rise only when each level of need has been satisfied;
- Herzberg's (1966) 'motivators', which he ranked in response to questions about job satisfaction, and in which 'job interest' came first.

These theories are quite closely linked. A manager, having thought carefully about what motivates those with whom they manage, may also think about how to motivate further those who do not seem to be working as well as they might. It is the manager's responsibility to make sure that the members of the team are truly motivated. Here is a motivation checklist which might be a helpful way of beginning to think about motivation and other people:

Activity

Motivation Checklist

Rate the extent to which you carry out the following approaches in motivating your team:

**5 = yes; 4 = to a great extent; 3 = to some extent;
2 = very little; 1 = no.**

1   Have you agreed with all your team their main targets and responsibilities, so that you can all recognize achievement?

2   Do you recognize the contribution of each member of the group and encourage other team members to do the same?

3   In the event of success do you acknowledge and build on it?

4   In the event of setbacks, do you identify what did go well, and give constructive guidance for improving future performance?

5   Do you delegate enough? Do you give adequate discretion over decisions and accountability to sub-groups or individuals?

6   Do you show those who work with you that you trust them? . . .

7   Or do you hedge them around with unnecessary controls?

8   Does your team have adequate opportunity for professional development?

9   Do you encourage all members of the team to develop their capacities to the full?

10   Is the overall performance of each member regularly reviewed in face-to-face discussion?

11   Do you make sufficient time to talk and listen, so that you understand the unique (and changing) profile of needs and wants in each person, so that you are able to work comfortably with them?

12   Do you positively encourage able people to seek promotion either within or outside their present institution?

There are some useful suggestions contained within these questions for managers to think about if it seems that a team member is unmotivated. A list might be drawn up of what a manager thinks counts towards her or his own motivation. It is then interesting to list what the manager thinks motivates those for whom they have management responsibility, and to compare these two lists! It is probable that managers place their own motivators on a higher Maslow level than they place the motivators for those who are managed. Some of the strategies in the list in the previous block are contained within effective appraisal systems, especially when attention is paid to power balances and to ensuring that it is really safe for two-way conversations. Delegation is also mentioned here; when done well it is a great motivator.

Delegation

Many people say that they cannot delegate, partly because they have nobody to delegate to, and partly because if they had someone, the necessary explanation would take too long: 'it's quicker if I do it myself'. In many ways managers are reluctant to delegate aspects of their work either because they see delegation as a way of getting rid of unwanted and unglamorous tasks, or because they believe that they should work harder than other people (as the more highly-paid manager) and so are honour-bound not to get rid of any tasks.

Both these explanations miss out a very important aspect of delegation — it is an ideal strategy for encouraging professional development. It could be that this educative aspect is often forgotten because management books link notions of delegation with time management. This is misleading: it is also a very skilled and constructive activity when done properly, and needs commitment and understanding from the manager who is doing the delegating — it is not to be undertaken lightly.

Activity

Delegation

This activity can be done in groups of three or four, and depends on using about an hour to work through the answers and definitions asked for:

1 Define in one sentence:
   i.   Instruction
   ii.   Delegation
   iii. Abdication

2 What are the positive and negative factors in delegation (up to three of each)
   i.   for delegators
   ii.   for delegatees?

3 How should you delegate
   i.   before delegation
   ii.   when delegating
   iii. during the task
   iv.   after the task?

4 Under normal circumstances, what should be delegated?

5 Under normal circumstances, what should not be delegated?

Anne Gold (1998) writes that the outcomes of this activity may include that:

- beliefs about teambuilding and working with people will inform the planning about delegating: if the aim is to develop and support colleagues into acquiring the expertise to perform tasks they could not perform previously, the process of productive delegation is a most useful framework.

- In order to delegate productively, it is necessary to negotiate carefully with the people to whom the delegator wishes to delegate. Delegation is neither dumping horrible tasks on subordinates, nor briskly telling someone what to do. It requires the use of careful listening skills with which the delegator ensures that both the delegator and the delegatee really understand each other, so that misunderstandings can be dealt with, and so that an agreement is reached about the process which both can sustain until the task is completed.

- Effective delegation is *not* principally a way of saving time; at least, not initially. In order to delegate fairly, the initial discussions need to take enough time to make sure that everyone concerned has agreed both the content of the delegation and the process of the delegation. This is because the transaction may well be set up to fail unless it is carefully agreed, planned and monitored.

- It may be that the delegated tasks are ones that the delegator could have done faster and more successfully alone. And some of the tasks left with the head of department may be ones which are boring and mundane. Delegating is not about getting rid of jobs people dislike doing. In selecting the tasks to be delegated, it is helpful to be reminded of underlying principles about management. And eventually, the support and encouragement of the team will entail less work, because other team members are supporting the team as well.

- It is important to examine decisions about which tasks can be delegated. Issues of power and habit encourage us to cling to some tasks which are developmental for other people, and of which a handover could eventually ease a manager's load. For example, chairing meetings. Is it customary for the head of department to chair all departmental meetings? Is it the custom for the most senior or powerful staff member to chair relevant meetings? Is this necessary? Here is an example where custom often dictates unnecessary practice. And careful delegation of the chairing role could ease the load of the teamleader while developing important skills in the rest of the team.

Managing Stress

This is another problem that is to be recognized both in managers and in those they manage and to be taken care of by managers. In other words, managers have a responsibility to be aware of when they are stressed themselves, and of when those they manage are stressed. George Orwell (cited in Bott, 1958) describes stress very well. Although he is describing it in a writer, not a teacher, there are common elements to both:

It is now (1949) sixteen years since my first book was published, and about twenty-one years since I started publishing articles in the magazines. Throughout that time there has literally been not one day in which I did not feel I was idling, that I was behind with the current job, and that my total output was miserably small. Even at the periods when I was working ten hours a day on a book, or turning out four or five articles a week, I have never been able to get any sense of achievement out of the work that is actually in progress because it always goes slower than I intend, and in any case I feel that a book or even an article does not exist until it is finished. But as soon as a book is finished, I begin, actually from the next day, worrying because the next one is not begun.

It does not seem, in reading this extract, that Orwell found stress so paralysing that he could not work. Nevertheless, he did find it constantly painful and depressing, and with his descriptive skills he presents an easily recognized condition. There are many other symptoms of stress, which Jack Dunham (1992) calls 'reactions to stress', and some of which he groups into:

behavioural – for example, heavy smoking, driving too fast and an inability to sit still and relax;

emotional – which might include a general feeling that the workload is too heavy and depression;

mental – where teachers report a need for constant self-control, not enough time to reflect, and fear of poor judgment;

physical – which includes headaches, difficulty breathing, poor sleep patterns, indigestion, and palpitations. (p. 92)

It is important to recognize reactions to stress in both self and others, and for managers to acknowledge that what is genuinely stressful for some people may hardly affect others, and vice versa. The Education Service Advisory Committee published a booklet (1990) which included some views from staff about causes of stress:

In teaching, stress is brought about by so many petty and unrelated factors; one never has control of all the relevant facts to bring about a solution to a problem.

The constant demands on non-teaching time make it extremely difficult just to keep pace, let alone innovate or experiment.

The sense of isolation causes stress — being trapped between school management, who are less than impressive, and the pupils.

Once, teachers were well respected in society. Today it is as if we were working against and in spite of society. (p. 8)

This booklet was written just after the introduction of the Education Reform Act, before the National Curriculum and ensuing bureaucratic demands were fully in operation in the UK. It is not surprising that the DfEE recently funded research into whether the pressures of growing bureaucratic demands on teachers are causing pressure or stress, and whether they are affecting the level of teaching and learning.

In order to try to predict what may cause stress and what may not in team members, it would be helpful here to examine the differences between stress and pressure. It is acknowledged that there is a continuum flowing along a necessary-pressure-for-performance line where the two ends are 'bored and frustrated' and 'over-stressed'. In other words, if there is no pressure at all, people are so bored they cannot function, and if there is too much pressure, they are so stressed that they cannot function. Dunham (1992, p. 95) shows the most effective performance of tasks comes with a certain level of pressure: just after pressure is seen as a challenge, and before the early warning signs of anxiety and irritability. An effective manager can gauge with team members the level of pressure needed for the most effective performance of each team member, and it will be different for everyone.

The Education Service Advisory Committee (1990) defines stress as

> a process that can occur when there is an unresolved mismatch between the perceived pressures of the work situation and an individual's inability to cope. (p. 3)

We would like to add that an unresolved mismatch between a personal philosophy of education and the organization's educational philosophy to the recipe for stress. Torrington and Weightman (1989, pp. 51–60) suggest an engrossing task which allows school staff to compare their own beliefs about managing and organizing a school with those that are published about the organizational beliefs. The outcomes of the task show that as long as the individuals and the organization are in agreement about the way decisions are made, the choice of organizational structure is not important. In other words, for those who work in a school which is managed in a way that is at serious odds with the beliefs of the individuals in the school, stress and dysfunction will soon be manifested.

If, therefore, many of the stressors coming from working in a school are due to the way the institution is organized, there are clearly basic organizational responsibilities lying with the senior managers to find ways of drawing individual beliefs closer to those of the whole school. If senior managers do not take this responsibility, is it possible for middle managers to become more reflective and take on this responsibility themselves?

Conclusion

There are many more management skills, not mentioned here, that good managers use automatically, carefully and regularly. It is necessary, however, to examine *why* such skills are employed: without a sense of purpose and clear values, these skills are easily used to manipulate those who are being managed. Teachers are, rightly, swift to suspect exploitation, but they are also quick to recognize poor management skills and to applaud effective ones. Good interpersonal skills combined with sound strategic planning capabilities and underpinned by shared values are welcomed in all schools.

References

Ball, S. (1994) *Education Reform*, Buckingham: Open University Press.

Bell, L. (1992) *Managing Teams in Secondary Schools*, London: Routledge.

Blase, J. and Blase, J. (1994) *Empowering Teachers*, California: Corwin Press.

Bott, G. (Ed) (1958) *Selected Writings of George Orwell*, London: Heinemann Educational.

Caldwell, B. and Spinks, J. (1988) *The Self-Managing School*, London: Falmer.

Dunham, J. (1992 second edition) *Stress in Teaching*, London: Routledge.

Education Service Advisory Committee (1990) *Managing Occupational Stress: A Guide for Managers and Teachers in the Schools Sector*, London: HMSO.

Everard, K.B. and Morris, G. (1996 edition) *Effective School Management*, London: Paul Chapman Publishing.

Fidler, B. (1996) *Strategic Planning for School Improvement*, London: Pitman Publishing.

Gold, A. (1998) *Head of Department: Principles in Practice*, London: Cassell.

Hargreaves, D. and Hopkins, D. (Eds) (1994) *Development Planning for School Improvement*, London: Cassell.

Herzberg, F. (1966) *Work and the Nature of Man*, Cleveland, Ohio: World Publishing.

Kenway, J. and Fitzclarence, L. (1997) 'Masculinity, violence and schooling: challenging "poisonous pedagogies",' *Gender and Education*, **9**, 1, March 1997.

Maslow, A.H. (1943) 'A theory of human motivation', *Psychological Review*, **50**.

Torrington, D. and Weightman, J. (1989) *Management and Organization in Secondary Schools: A Training Handbook*, Oxford: Blackwell.

Chapter 5

Working with People, Part Two — Developing Staff

Key issues for managers:

- who does the term 'staff' include?

- staff selection and recruitment

- staff induction

- continuing professional development

- appraisal

- career development

- the HRM approach

The following case studies are presented in order to offer a focus for these key professional development issues for managers. The first task, in the box at the end of these descriptions of teachers, includes questions which are intended to begin these explorations.

Ronald Diamond BSc, aged 24, is a talented teacher with two years' experience in a comprehensive school with falling rolls, in a deprived inner city area. He has a rather poor Physics degree, strongly held political beliefs and he chose to teach in a school with severe social problems. Despite his limited experience he has volunteered to be a staff representative on the Parent Teacher Association — a role he carries out with charm and energy. He is also a local councillor and a member of a pressure group called 'EM — Education for the Majority'. His pamphlet, 'Our Schools', has been used by local radio in programmes dealing with the effects of government education policy. He is actively involved in a variety of community projects.

He is a charismatic teacher who appears to have potential. His teaching is slapdash and lessons are not well-prepared, but the children love him, and he is well-liked by his colleagues and the technicians despite his total lack of organization and failure to meet deadlines. Aware of the value of his shortage subject, Ronald Diamond expects rapid promotion, and sees himself in a very few years, as a young, radical and vigorous headteacher.

Joyce Fletcher BEd, is 45 years old. Until two years ago she was the Special Educational Needs Co-ordinator (CPS + 2 Responsibility Points) in a primary school.

She provided in-class support and small group withdrawal sessions for all the children with Special Educational Needs in the school, developed and managed the Special Educational Needs policy and was seen by her colleagues as being very effective. As the result of the introduction of a whole school Special Educational Needs Policy prompted by reduced resources, Joyce found herself teaching a difficult class full-time, as well as retaining the curriculum responsibility for children with special educational needs in the school. She is having great difficulty adjusting to the demands of managing a whole class, and at the same time, feels she is failing the children who really need her help. She is now quite depressed, and sees little hope for her own professional future. She saw herself as a good SEN support teacher, and now appears totally de-skilled as a classroom teacher.

Margaret Smith MSc, aged 30 has a CPS + 2 responsibility points allowance as number three in the mathematics department of a popular and thriving comprehensive school. She has a good Mathematics degree, is ambitious and hard-working, takes all her responsibilities seriously and gets on well with the pupils. Twice recently she has been passed over for more senior roles in the department — most recently when she applied for the post of head of department. She is a bright teacher with considerable latent powers of organization. She is full of interesting ideas, but the limitations of her responsibility (largely for the lower level classes in years 10 and 11), and the fact that her two senior colleagues are very able and recently appointed, reduce her chances of promotion.

She is of Caribbean origin, and was born and has lived all her life in the UK. She increasingly feels that she has been the victim of prejudice. As a well-qualified mathematician she thinks she might have greater opportunities outside teaching and is seriously considering leaving the profession.

Activity

For each of these case-studies imagine that you are a newly appointed head of department or headteacher. Think about each case in turn and consider:

a. How you would work with, and how you would try to help the development of each teacher?

b. What are the whole-school staff development issues raised by each case?

Who Does the Term 'Staff' Include?

Books about school management generally seem to take for granted that 'staff' means teaching staff. Here, we are referring to any of the adults who are paid to work in the school, and in particular those who are connected with learning and teaching in the school. Classroom assistants and laboratory technicians, lunchtime supervisors and schoolkeeping staff come into constant contact with the children, and they influence and are influenced by the ethos of the school. Many of these staff members have far less access to professional development than teaching staff, often because they are paid by the hour. Some of them are not invited to staff meetings which can be an ideal medium for staff development when well run, and several of them would not like to be expected to attend these meetings. We suggest that schools think carefully about the development of *all* members of staff, and where possible, remember that non-teaching staff can be those people with a great deal of influence over the young people in a school. Seifert (1996, p. 127) writes that the essential issue is that the failure to treat all staff equally is a waste of resources as well as being wrong.

Staff Selection and Recruitment

Recruitment procedures in the UK are bound by an equal opportunities legislative framework which covers gender, race and disability. This framework includes laws on equal pay and on sex and race discrimination, which are general to all employers, and are laid out for headteachers in the Croner Guides (updated each year). Because this information can be accessed easily elsewhere, we will not go into detail here. This section of Chapter 6 will pay attention to the principles underpinning fair and just staff selection and recruitment procedures.

Chapter 3 introduced team roles, and we suggested there that the most useful people in a team may be just the ones who because of their skills, qualities and attributes, find it most difficult to tolerate and work with each other. This social psychology explanation of the importance of understanding and working with differences links with the sociological and ethical work done on equal opportunities in the field of education in the UK in the 1980s. Before then, many people who worked in teams looked for a replacement for a departing team member through the equivalent of old boys' networks: they looked for people who fitted the space left exactly, and who would do so without causing friction or disturbance.

The equal opportunities recruitment procedures introduced by most UK local education authorities in the 1980s were based on an understanding that people should not be appointed because of whom they knew, or because they simply had a similar background to the rest of the team, or because they would put up least resistance to the running of the team. Rather they would be appointed because they had a professional background and experience which would enrich the team's productivity, and because they could offer qualities which other members lack. The different approach to problem-solving this might bring would probably be because the new team members were not necessarily part of the dominant discourse of education — white, male and middle class. Indeed, it was after the introduction of these procedures that many inner city schools appointed more women teachers and managers, and more teachers and leaders from ethnic minorities who became important role models for the young people in inner city schools.

There were some problems with the new procedures — it would be impossible to make a precise science out of something so imprecise as human interaction. Many skilled recruiters regretted the loss of reliance on their intuition or hunches; but intuition is socially constructed and culturally biased. Others felt that the rigidity of the process meant the suppression of important evidence; but the best recruitment procedures allow for the disclosure of relevant evidence — they are not clandestine. Certainly they are an improvement on the previous procedures, as the statistics of increased access to power of women and people from ethnic minorities show.

Some of the lessons learnt from these equal opportunities selection procedures are very important ones, and many schools still base their own recruitment procedures firmly on this work. But the independence and freedom of choice given to individual schools by the 1988 and subsequent Education Acts (see Chapter 6) mean that only those schools which are deeply committed to issues of equity put their principles into practice through their recruitment procedures. Before 1988, local authorities took a lead role in the maintenance and monitoring of these procedures, and if they have been diluted, it is because the power of the local authority to influence schools so closely has been curtailed. Grant-maintained schools have no links with the local education authority in matters of recruitment, and those schools which are required to work closely with their local authority must pay for the attendance at meetings of the Clerk to the Governors and for their support with paperwork. Many governing bodies have subsequently chosen not to 'buy in' the services of the Clerk, or do so only periodically. In this way regular attendance by representatives of the local authority at recruitment boards is no longer expected, and so regular advice and local authorities values are no longer so accessible.

Activity

If your school has a published recruitment policy, read it while attempting to answer the following questions:

- are there any direct allusions to equity?
- does the policy include the school's equal opportunities policy or quotations from it, or references to it?
- does the policy include the school's statement of values and show ways in which these values are echoed in the policy?
- does the policy insist that members of the recruitment panel have received training in recruitment procedures?
- does the policy suggest that the recruitment panel pays attention to its gender and race balance?
- is the same group of panel members responsible for drawing up the job description, the advertisement, the short list and the interview questions, so that they are committed to the whole procedure and so that they understand how it all fits together?
- does the policy include guidelines for the actual interview which lay emphasis on creating an atmosphere to encourage the interviewee to interview well?

Readers of this chapter may take it for granted that the three teachers at the beginning were recruited fairly, and that their schools were pleased to employ them.

Staff Induction

It is likely that some members of staff at Ronald Diamond's school are having difficulty with him because his school or departmental induction programmes have not been effective for him. Such programmes are a way of initiating new staff members into the culture and ethos of a school so that they both share it and contribute to it actively. Some schools pay a great deal of attention to newly qualified and beginning teachers (NQTs), using induction procedures to encourage them to become reflective practitioners who think about their professional practice and relationships so that they eventually become enmeshed into the culture of the school. Far fewer schools have the resources to do this work with experienced teachers who are new to the organization, or with those like Joyce Fletcher, whose job description and subsequent status change *within* the school.

It is clear that NQTs (those people who are newly qualified as teachers) are more vulnerable to influence while developing a set of professional expectations and strategies. Ken Jones and Peter Stammers (1997) write:

> NQTs often find their beliefs vigorously challenged as they attempt to meet the demands and expectations pressed upon them by schools and the dialectic process of induction reshapes the actions and beliefs of both the individual and the school. NQTs change as they affiliate with an institution and the organisation changes as new members usher in fresh ideas and unique ways of acting. It is during those first crucial, formative years (and none more so than that first year) that a teacher must be helped to form appropriate 'skills' and 'habits' and struggle against the tendency to fall back on mere instruction and control. (pp. 87–88)

It appears from his case study that Ronald Diamond has not had access to, or has resisted any attempts to give him access to, possibilities for the formation of appropriate skills and habits. His energy, his commitment to education and his excellent professional relationships have not been directed by his school into patterns and habits that make the most of them. If his department had clear and shared guidelines about lesson preparation and record keeping, and if those with management responsibility for him had helped him organize himself better, there would be little basis for the complaints about him. A successful induction programme and clear role modelling within his department would not only help him to develop those skills and habits, but would also help him understand why he might harness all his impressive qualities and channel them into being a truly professional teacher.

It may be argued that Joyce Fletcher's school had a responsibility, because of the marked change in her job description, to induct her into her new role. A sensitive management team might have developed an individual induction programme for her, which might cover, for example, the period before she took over her class and in the first year after. It might include:

- visits to other teachers in her school and to classes in other schools to look at ways of organizing classes before she began working with her own class full-time;
- discussions about classroom management issues both before and after she became a class teacher;
- and a mentor system or a support group through which she could reflect on some of her classroom difficulties to make sense of them and plan strategies to alleviate those difficulties.

Whichever induction methods were chosen to suit Ronald Diamond and Joyce Fletcher, it is clear that responsibility for their adaptation to be more productive and successful within their schools lies with their managers as well as with themselves. It is not helpful simply to blame them for not being good enough.

Continuing Professional Development

A reading of recent publications about education management will show that writing about staff development has evolved into writing about continuing professional development. This writing attempts to find answers to the following questions: in what ways might those with management responsibility for a school ensure that all the staff in the school subscribe to the same set of expectations, or that the school ethos is contributed to by the whole staff? How might those who work in a school make sure that they always deliver the best learning and teaching possible? In what ways might a school continue to be an educative organization for *all* those people who work there?

'Continuing professional development' implies that development *carries on* for all staff throughout their professional careers, and that the outcomes of effective development contribute to the professional activity of the organization — the delivery of learning and teaching. The following main management issues make for an effective continuing professional development policy:

- those who manage the policy need an understanding of theories which underpin *adult learning*;
- the school will have the broadest possible set of strategies to encourage *continuous professional development*;
- there is a shared understanding about the *balance of individual professional development needs with those of the school.*

Understanding How Adults Learn

There are three writers who have contributed to the understanding of adult learning: David Kolb (1984), who wrote about experiential learning; Stephen Brookfield (1987), who writes about developing critical thinking; and Donald Schön (1991), who wrote about the development of the reflective practitioner. All three of them are influential in the continuing professional development of teachers because they are concerned with the autonomy of the adult learner, and they suggest ways of helping adult learners make sense of previous professional experiences. According to Kolb (1984) a teacher will do so by discussion, by reflection and by reading, and will then decide on the necessary adjustments to practice next time, and will subsequently begin to plan ways of putting those changes into practice. And then, after the experience of new practice, the practitioner will reflect once again on the outcomes of those changes in practice.

Brookfield (1987) suggests that teachers who are learning more about learning and teaching may do so through critical thinking. He writes about critical thinking as a learning conversation:

1. Good conversations are reciprocal and involving:
in a good conversation, the participants are continually involved in the process; they are either talking or listening. Developing critical thinking is a process in which listening and contributing are of equal importance.

2. The course of good conversations cannot be anticipated:
when we begin to ask people to identify assumptions underlying their habitual ways of thinking and learning, we do not know exactly how they are going to respond.

3. Good conversations entail diversity and agreement:
a measure of diversity, disagreement, and challenge is central to helping people to think critically. Unless we accept that people have views very different from ours, and that a multiplicity of interpretations of practically every idea or action is possible, we will be unable to contemplate alternatives in our own thoughts and actions. (pp. 238–241)

A manager who takes the management responsibility of developing staff seriously will have thought about ways in which tired and hardworking teachers are best encouraged to develop their professional skills. The three subjects of the case studies are people who already have professional experience to draw on in order to develop new strategies for learning and teaching. They may each be sensitive about their learning needs, and Brookfield's learning conversations are careful and respectful ways of working together.

Strategies to Encourage Continuous Professional Development

It is possible to think of professional development as an activity which is severely limited by resourcing. In other words, some teachers think that they can only learn more about their work if they are sent on expensive courses. In certain circumstances, off-site courses are indeed helpful and productive. But the majority of successful professional development happens through the daily discussions and interactions in a school: curriculum leaders and managers ensure that practitioners think and talk and read about their work and their learning and teaching in order to make sense of what is happening. It is necessary to pay attention to the atmosphere of professional talk in a school: good meetings are informative places where learning happens, and discussions in corridors and planned visits to classrooms are stimulating as well. In this way, the school becomes a learning organization.

Both Ronald Diamond and Joyce Fletcher would probably develop their teaching and classroom management skills more constructively in schools and staffrooms where all staff discussed teaching and learning as a matter of course, and where difficulties, new ideas and newspaper articles are shared without rancour or competition.

> **Activity**
> Either alone or with some colleagues, take a large piece of paper, in the centre of which is written **continuous professional development**.
>
> Brainstorm all the possible activities and strategies that you can think of which encourage the talk and thought that help teachers to develop their work.
>
> Then mark off those which already take place in your school.
>
> Choose at least one more strategy or activity which you have written in your brainstorm, and think about ways in which you might introduce this to your school in the near future.

Balancing Individual Professional Development Needs with Those of the School

In Chapter 1, we referred to John Adair's (1986) diagram in which he shows that teams work best when attention is paid to the careful balance of the needs of individual team members, the task and the needs of the institution. The same balance of needs, indeed the same diagram, is helpful when thinking about planning for continuing professional development. If professional development plans are driven by the needs of the institution, individual staff members may not feel as though their particular development needs are addressed; if the needs of the task are paramount (for example, working with the urgency of action planning after an OfSTED inspection) other institutional development plans may be subsumed or even lost within the development planning which has superseded all original plans and needs.

There are times when individual development needs appear to override the needs of the team: a team which contains Ronald Diamond may be compelled to pay attention to his lack of planning and organizational strategies before it can spend time on other team developments. However, the team leader is likely to have longer term planning which takes timing into account. They will know that when Ronald has been helped to plan more constructively, the team will be more able to benefit from his energy and creativity, and he in turn may be able to offer his services to other members of the team.

Appraisal

Garrett and Bowles (1997) show how individual development can fit into whole school development and improvement:

> One mechanism we have to hand is appraisal . . . the best type of appraisal is one which encompasses a formative development function and is linked to professional development resourcing. At the same time, it is to be recognised that there is an accountability function to appraisal which is satisfied in the best cases by supported goal-setting and effective follow-up. (p. 32)

In other words, an appraisal system is one way of negotiating the balance of needs between the individual, the team and the organization.

Appraisal systems are to be found at different stages in many schools. Appraisal is an example of an initially well-planned initiative which foundered because it was under-resourced at the implementation phase: careful discussions between employers and unions led to well-evaluated pilot schemes which were then disseminated in several effective ways. Teachers were excited by the prospect of careful appraisal, and appraisal training was well under way before it became clear that the money necessary to resource appraisal schemes sufficiently would not be forthcoming. Subsequently, schools which are committed to continuing professional development have worked out appraisal systems which are based on the belief that appraisal is a vital part of professional development. There is still cynicism about appraisal but this is most often in schools that do not clearly base their system on a set of beliefs about equal power in the appraisal transaction, or where appraisal outcomes do not seem to lead to any changes in conditions of work or in professional development planning.

The following safeguards may be incorporated into an appraisal scheme to ensure that appraisees really do have the chance to contribute seriously to their professional development needs:

- *confidentiality* — in many appraisal schemes, only a summary of agreed targets is passed on to the headteacher and chair of governors by the appraiser. In this way, confidentiality is ensured within the interview; the appraiser will not talk to anyone else about the fears and expectations raised by the appraisee and so the latter is able to explore all issues about professional practice;

- *(within limits) a choice of appraiser* — it should be possible to ask for another appraiser if an appraisee is not happy with the suggested one. In small schools, this may be more difficult, but hidden agendas and long-term personality differences must not cloud the process. The appraisee must have the opportunity to choose someone with whom they can work within the appraisal scheme, and preferably someone who fully understands the professional activities with which they are involved;

- *attention paid to the setting (time and place) for the appraisal dialogues* — a mutually agreed space is to be chosen, one which is at least as comfortable for the appraisee as for the appraiser. Care is taken over such things as the placing of chairs, the silencing of phones and the closing of doors, all of which ensure that the appraisee is interviewed carefully without interruptions. The appraiser also makes sure that enough time is given for a careful interview and discussion;

- *negotiated classroom observation* — if this part of the process is handled really well, the appraisee will have an ideal opportunity for clear and professional feedback about teaching: the feedback will be non-judgmental but encouraging. Agreed focus will include highlighting areas to be developed, and will pay attention to an aspect of teaching chosen by the appraisee;

- *negotiated targets* — the professional development targets framed as an outcome of the classroom observation and the interview will not be dictated by the appraiser, but will be negotiated and mutually agreed, with reference however to the balance of needs of the team and the task, as well as the individual teachers. Only after this careful process will targets be recorded and transmitted, without names, to senior management;

- *and joint training* — when appraisers and appraisees receive appraisal training together, there is no opportunity for secrecy or for alternative plans and arrangements. There will be no hidden agendas, and the appraisee as well as the appraiser will know what can be expected of the process.

Activity

Look at the description of the appraisal system in your school, or in a school you know:

To what extent is there evidence of any of the previous strategies?

Can you trace the power balances within the published system?

Do you think that the appraisee will feel free to explore professional problems and possibilities?

Are there clear links published between the appraisal process and the professional development scheme in the school?

All three case study subjects would benefit from an appraisal system that was able to take their professional needs into account while balancing them with their school's needs:

- In a more helpful setting, *Ronald Diamond* would already have worked within a suitable induction programme and would have been offered professional development opportunities which address his organizational problems. An effective appraisal system would allow him to feed back his views about the organization while negotiating a realistic professional future, and to develop strategies to achieve his professional aims.

- Within an appraisal system, *Joyce Fletcher* might well have found a way of agreeing and planning for a much more productive transition to a different position in her school. She might have been able to negotiate her future role and her development for it, and have used the appraisal system to monitor and feed back how she was doing and how helpful she was finding the support strategies. Her agreed targets would have made her transition much more manageable and supported, and her self-confidence would not have been allowed to dissolve so utterly.

- A truly effective appraisal scheme would have allowed *Margaret Smith* to have more input into the planning of her career in her school. She would not have found herself locked into having constant responsibility for one group of young people to the detriment of her career, and she would have had the forum for constructive career decision-making and planning. She would also have been able to show how the school appeared to have made sure that her talents were underrated.

Career Development

Appraisal schemes offer a formal opportunity for discussions about career development in ways that were not previously so clear. Before appraisal systems were so commonplace, some managers in schools only discussed career planning (especially to move on to another school) if they wanted to encourage less successful staff members to leave. Career development was seen too often as moving to another school. It may well be a constructive move, and may be important for the teacher who moves, but it is not always so for the manager: it is often disappointing when a team leader builds up a team which performs really well, only to lose a key and effective team member to an outside promotion.

It may not be necessary to move away from a school for constructive career development, however. Margaret Smith's career would develop more creatively if she were given other responsibilities within the maths department, or if she were encouraged to take on other cross-curricular or pastoral responsibilities within the school. A manager who valued Margaret's work and took responsibility generally for career development would not wait until she became disenchanted with her position. Schools that have an ethos of learning and constant development would also ensure that staff members were making and following career plans if they so wished.

The Human Resource Management (HRM) Approach

Riches (1997) writes:

> HRM is all about the improvement of performance or productivity — however problematical these may be to define — through the effective use of human resources; always acknowledging that humans in an organisation are the most important part of getting things done. People need to be managed to optimise their own and institutional performance and value being managed. No one gains from an *ad hoc* approach to managing people; to ignore them, to treat them as pawns on an institutional chess board is neither ethical nor liberal nor any assistance towards performance. (p. 20)

Undoubtedly, those who are managed deserve to be taken note of, and to be helped to make the most of their efforts, but some of the language Riches uses to argue this must be used with care in education. He writes about 'productivity', and 'optimising own and institutional performance', both of which are terms that seem to rely too heavily on outcomes which are difficult to measure when the human relations of learning and teaching are taken into account. To measure these outcomes in terms of productivity and performance would mean reducing extremely complicated and necessarily nuanced activities to the equivalent of tick boxes. And so the complicated and multi-layered arena of learning and teaching is reduced to a monodimensional measurable plateau.

The term 'Human Resource Management' is linked with the Total Quality Management movement. We have looked at some of the problems with TQM in Chapter 3, where we reminded readers that the basic principles of quality management are the basic principles of all good management, but that they sometimes lack a values-based framework that is focused particularly on educational needs. The same criticism may be true of some of the writing about HRM: the strategies suggested for managing people efficiently are helpful, but they are not always tuned clearly enough to basic values which inform ethical management in education.

This is not an argument against managing people in an organization. It is rather an argument against finding strategies and systems to manage in a controlled and measurable form, and then broadcasting those measurements in order to persuade people that progress has taken place. The problem is that the efficacy of the strategies, systems, measurement and progress are unexamined and undisputed, so that ethics, values, creativity and contestation of uneasy terrain are masked or silenced.

Conclusion

We are not suggesting that managers should learn about and use a series of management techniques that control and dampen down the debates and uncomfortable feelings that are the byproducts of creative learning and teaching. Rather, we urge managers to make sure that they take an actively developmental responsibility for the members of staff with whom they work. This developmental responsibility is underpinned by fair and just selection and employment procedures, an understanding of adult learning, and a commitment to continuous professional development.

References

ADAIR, J. (1986) *Effective Teambuilding*, Reading: Pan.

BOLAM, R., MCMAHON, A., POCKLINGTON, K. and WEINDLING, D. (1993) *Effective Management in Schools*, London: HMSO.

BROOKFIELD, S.A. (1987) *Developing Critical Thinkers*, Milton Keynes: Open University Press.

CRONER'S GUIDES (1997 and updated every year) *The Head's Legal Guide*, New Malden: Croner Publication Limited.

GARRETT, V. with BOWLES, C. (1997) 'Teaching as a profession: The role of professional development' in TOMLINSON, H. (Ed) *Managing Continuing Professional Development in Schools*, London: BEMAS/Paul Chapman Publishing.

JONES, K. and STAMMERS, P. (1997) 'The early years of the teacher's career: Induction into the profession' in TOMLINSON, H. (Ed) *Managing Continuing Professional Development in Schools*, London: Paul Chapman Publishing.

KOLB, D.A. (1984) *Experiential Learning*, New Jersey: Prentice Hall.

RICHES, C. (1997) 'Managing for people and performance' in BUSH, T. and MIDDLEWOOD, D. (Eds) *Managing People in Education*, London: Paul Chapman Publishing.

SCHÖN, D.A. (1991) *Educating the Reflective Practitioner*, San Francisco: Jossey-Bass.

SEIFERT, R. (1996) *Human Resource Management in Schools*, London: Pitman.

Chapter 6

Managing in the Market Place

Key issues for managers:

- is competition or collaboration the best way forward for schools?

- what are the implications of the change in the balance of power and responsibility between school management, governors and the government?

- how can the school effectively meet the needs of all its students?

- how can the school deal with issues of parental choice?

- how can the school market itself in a socially responsible way?

The Legislative Framework

The legal and administrative framework within which managers in schools are working has changed beyond all recognition since the Education Reform Act of 1988. Before that, schools were managed within a 'triangle of tension', set up by the 1944 Education Act, between central government in the shape of the minister and the Department of Education and Science (DES); the local education authorities (LEAs) in the shape of elected members and LEA officers; and, the senior management in schools. This was essentially a bureaucratic framework which, it was claimed by the government and its advisers, stifled initiative and made it difficult to raise standards or to introduce new ideas.

The main charges against the system set up by the 1944 Education Act were:

- the education system was fragmented and standards across the country varied widely, which was unacceptable;

- LEAs had too much power, and used it to force schools to introduce ideologically motivated reforms, such as 'anti-racist' initiatives which were not acceptable to the government or to parents;

- LEAs and schools were 'producer-dominated', that is, schools and LEAs were being run for the benefit of those working in them, and not for the benefit of parents and children;

- the decision-making processes between schools and LEAs were over-bureaucratic and slow, so that schools were not able to take decisions about how best to use resources to achieve their aims;

- parents had little choice about which school their children should attend and therefore schools had no incentive to improve their performance;

- the 'secret garden' of the curriculum was controlled by schools, to a large extent, and also by LEAs, so that parents and the wider community, had very little say over what went on in schools;

- LEAs and schools were not oriented sufficiently towards the world of work and did not take into account the views of employers about what the purposes of education should be.

Activity
You may wish to take some time here, to reflect upon these criticisms of the pre-1988 situation, and ask whether they were justified and whether the current organization of education has overcome the problem.

The 1988 Education Reform Act, together with other legislation during the 1980s and 1990s, was geared towards changing the purposes, governance and accountability systems, and the content of schooling. The fundamental change was from a system of bureaucratic control through LEAs, which contained elements of democratic accountability, to a market-driven system, where accountability and control are exercised, to a much greater extent, through the power of parents acting as consumers. The steps through which this was achieved are detailed below:

1980 The 1980 Education Act gave parents limited rights to choose a school and to appeal to an LEA Appeals Panel if they did not get the school of their choice. LEAs were not allowed to alter significantly the planned admissions limits of schools without the Secretary of State for Education's permission. It also required the publication of exam results (GCE, CSE and later GCSE).

1986 The 1986 Education Act No 2 changed the balance of representation on governing bodies to include more parents and also teacher governors and to reduce the proportion of LEA nominees. Members of the local community could be co-opted.

1988 Education Reform Act introduced the National Curriculum; Standard Attainment Tasks; local management of schools; grant maintained status; formula funding of schools; more open enrolment; abolished the Inner London Education Authority; introduced the publication of league tables.

1991 Teachers Pay and Conditions Act — set up Teachers' Pay Review Body. Abolished the role of the unions and employers in pay negotiations.

1992 FE and Sixth Form Colleges removed from LEA control and funded by the Higher Education Funding Council (HEFC), a non-elected body made up of people nominated by the government.

1992   Ofsted set up. Power to inspect schools removed from LEAs.

1993   Education Act, based on *Choice and Diversity* White Paper. This Act consolidated the reforms of the 1988 Act. It made it easier for schools to opt out of LEA control to become grant-maintained, it up-dated the 1981 legislation on special education; and it introduced the possibility for GM schools to select pupils on the basis of ability. The Funding Agency for Schools (FAS) (a non-elected body made up of people nominated by the government) set up to make decisions about funding and planning schools in LEAs where more than 10% of schools opted out.

1996   Education Act consolidated the changes introduced by these previous Acts, including incorporating aspects of the 1981 Act concerning children with special educational needs. It repealed much earlier legislation, including the 1944 Education Act, which had been the foundation of post-war education in Britain.

The new Labour government produced a White Paper, *Excellence in Schools*, in 1997, proposing some changes to the structures outlined above, but its main focus was 'on standards not structures' (DfEE, 1997). So essentially, the framework of competition, choice and public account-ability set up by successive Conservat-ive administrations in the 1980s and 1990s is set to remain.

What the changes brought about was the removal of power from locally elected and accountable LEAs and an increase in the power of parents, school management and governors on the one hand, and of central government, on the other. So an education system was cre-ated which was both more fragmented as schools became more diverse and socially divided, and also more stand-ardized, as the National Curriculum, test-ing and Ofsted inspections pushed schools towards uniformity.

> **Activity**
> Thinking of the schools which you are familiar with, make a list of the ways in which they have become more diverse and the ways in which they have become more standardized over the last five years.
>
> On balance, do you think there is more diversity or more uniformity in schools today?
>
> Thinking about the power balance between school management, gov-ernors, LEAs and central government, which group would you say has more power in schools today?

The Education Market

The United Kingdom has not been alone in its search for new ways of organizing its education system and the introduction of a market. Similar moves have been made in many of the developed countries, such as New Zealand, Australia, United States, and, to a lesser extent, mainland Europe. Lawton (1992) gives a number of reasons why this move has occurred in so many countries at around the same time.

A Loss of Confidence in Schools

Lawton calls this 'a legitimation crisis'. During the 1970s there was a sustained attack on the effectiveness of schools from a number of perspectives. Right wing commentators, such as the writers of the so-called 'Black Papers', criticized many aspects of the comprehensive system of schooling in England and Wales (Scottish comprehensives escaped these attacks and retained the confidence of parents, and in Northern Ireland a grammar school system remained in place). This 'discourse of derision' as it has been termed by the writers of a book which charts the rise of the Right wing attack on education (*Unpopular Education*, by the Centre for Contemporary Cultural Studies (CCCS, 1981)), undermined the status of teachers as a profession, attacked 'progressive' child-centred methods in primary teaching and mixed ability teaching in comprehensive schools. Despite a rise in the numbers of students taking 'O' and 'A' levels and going on to higher education, public perception was that standards were falling and that schools were failing. Similar views were found in many other developed countries, such as the USA, Australia and New Zealand.

From the Left, there were also criticisms that too many working-class children and children from ethnic minorities were failing in schools and that not enough was being done to ensure that children from these groups, as well as girls, achieved their potential. A number of (mainly Labour-controlled) LEAs put into practice equal opportunities policies to try to counteract these problems. These have had varying degrees of success, and, incidentally, led to criticisms from the Right that schools and LEAs are too politically motivated and that 'back to basics' was the way to improve the education system.

Concerns about Effectiveness

The criticisms of schools elaborated above are not without foundation. Measured against international standards, England and Wales have a poor record compared with many continental European countries, such as France, Germany and the Scandinavian countries. Fewer children are in school from the age of 16 than in almost any other European country. Fewer go on to higher education. International comparisons on achievement in maths and science show the UK slipping down international league tables.

These concerns are mirrored in the USA, where a national report — *A Nation at Risk* — graphically described a problematic future for the USA if standards were not improved. Part of the problem, it was argued, was that the over-bureaucratic system of school administration led to stagnation and a lack of accountability for improvement. Local management (or site-based management as it is called in the USA) was seen as one answer to the problem of lack of will to change.

Concerns about Efficiency

What has been called 'the fiscal crisis of the state' brought on by the oil crisis of the 1970s has led to calls for spending on social welfare to be curtailed. In many areas, including health, social services, housing and education, successive governments have sought efficiency savings. The UK government argued that LEAs were wasting money on an extensive bureaucracy in the town hall, and that a more efficient use of resources would be to delegate more money to schools and to let management within schools make decisions about how to use the resources to best effect. Similar reforms have been made in New Zealand and Australia and in some states in the USA and provinces in Canada.

The Managerial Revolution

In the commercial sector, many successful companies have subdivided their firms to create sub-units and have given managers freedom to achieve the company's object-ives in the way the managers think will be most effective. This 'tight ends, loose means' approach has been popularized by Peters and Waterman's (1982) book: *In Search of Excellence.* They suggest that successful managers should be held accountable for achieving objectives, not for following rules. An increased emphasis on the importance of school management competencies and the delegation of sig-nificant responsibilities to headteachers and governors suggest that the government is expecting this policy to achieve significant benefits in terms of raising educational standards and containing expenditure.

Parental Pressure

Lawton argues that parents of the current generation of school children — the 'baby boomers' of the post-war era, were much better educated than previous generations and are, therefore, much better informed and much more demanding of the system that educates their own children. A 'consumer ethic' among these parents means that they will want to have choices and to shop around to get the education they feel is right for their child. If there is no right of choice, parents will move house to be in the catchment area of the school they want. In multi-cultural societies, some groups will want to have schools which cater for their children and take account of their culture. This has happened in New Zealand, where Maori people have demanded their own schools, and in the United States where 'home schooling' has become a feature of the system in many states. In the USA, in particular, the Right-wing fundamentalist religious groups have been very influential in some areas of the country.

In practice, many of the explanations for the global phenomenon of re-structur-ing education systems appear to overlap. Economic crisis, concerns for efficiency, the rise of consumers' rights, over-bureaucratization, all interact with each other and have resulted in a move from the administration of schools within a centralized bureaucracy towards devolved management to the level of the school. In the UK this has been accompanied by open enrolment and formula funding of schools, which is a much more radical solution than that found in many other countries. It has also been accompanied by much tighter control from the centre of the content and delivery of the curriculum, something which many European countries have had for some time, but which does not yet exist in the USA, Canada or Australia. Neither do any other countries have accountability to consumers through the publica-tion of league tables of exam and test results.

Activity

Considering all the changes in the UK system described above, would you say that schools are now more tightly or more loosely controlled than under the pre-1988 system?

Make two lists: one of the ways in which the system is now tighter and one of the ways in which it is looser.

The version of education markets adopted in the UK is perceived as the most extreme devolution of power to 'the hidden hand of the market'. This reliance on market mechanisms is not confined to the education sector alone: the health service has been subjected to an even more rigorous form of market, through a range of devices such as General Practitioners (GP) fund-holding, opted out trust hospitals, league tables of hospitals etc. However, some commentators, such as LeGrand and Bartlett (1993) argue that markets in the public sector are not true markets, because they are highly regulated. They prefer to use the term: 'quasi-market' to characterize such public sector forms of organization.

> The distinguishing features of a quasi-market for a public service are the separation of purchaser from provider and an element of user choice between providers. The quasi-market remains highly regulated. The government continues to control such matters as entry by new providers, investment, the quality of the service (as with the National Curriculum), and the price, which is often zero to the user, as in schooling. (Levačić, 1995, p. 167)

The more extreme pro-market commentators have suggested that education should be completely left to market forces. James Tooley, for example, argues that there should be no state regulation or provision; that schooling should not be compulsory and that the content of schooling should not be prescribed. He also argues that taxes should be lowered and that parents should be asked to pay for their children's education from their increased disposable income (Tooley, 1996).

Activity

Is education without the state possible? If not, what degree of state intervention is desirable?

Make a list of those aspects of the organization of schooling which you think require state regulation.

Now list those aspects which should be left to the management of schools to decide.

How far do your lists coincide with the current division of powers and responsibilities between the government, LEAs and schools?

The Impact of Markets on Education

There has been a wide range of research carried out since the Education Reform Act and its successors, about education markets and their impact on schooling.

The government's claims were that markets would bring about the three 'Es' that were desirable for the provision of schooling: Efficiency, Economy and Effectiveness (Audit Commission, 1985). These three terms are taken from economic theory and can be defined as follows:

Efficiency   relates to achieving maximum output for a given input of resources.

Economy   relates to achieving an acceptable output for the minimum input of resources.

Effectiveness   relates to how well a given activity is achieving its established goals.

It can be seen that these three concepts are inter-related, but not necessarily congruent. Thus, a school's management of its resources could be efficient, but not effective. Or effective but not economic. One problem with applying these concepts to the outputs of schooling, is that there is no consensus about what these should be. The essence of the debate about the purposes of education, which is at the heart of many of the recent reforms, is about whether the primary goal of education is to enable every child to reach his or her potential, or whether it is to produce productive and responsible citizens. These two goals are not necessarily in opposition to each other, but when economic arguments such as those about efficiency, effectiveness and economy are introduced into the equation, the balance between achieving the maximum for each pupil and the need to operate within fixed budgets can be in conflict.

This leads to the consideration of another 'E' — Equity. Markets are not concerned with equitable outcomes for all. In fact, it is acknowledged that there are bound to be winners and losers in markets — this is the essence of a market economy. There are many definitions of equity and much confusion about what it means in educational terms. Tim Lee (1996) has explored these in his book *The Search for Equity*. Put simply, equity involves treating equals equally and un-equals unequally. In formula funding of schools, equity is practised by funding all children of the same age, at the same level (horizontal equity) but funding pupils of different ages at different levels (vertical equity), making the assumption that primary-aged pupils need fewer resources than secondary-aged ones. Vertical equity involves looking at outcomes and allocating resources on the basis of trying to ensure equitable outcomes for all. This version of equity is also practised, to some extent, by the allocation of extra resources to pupils with special needs, although the notional level of achievement towards which these extra resources is aimed is not well-defined. Nationally, of course, equitable funding of schooling is not achieved, since each LEA will set the level of funding for each age-group, and these vary widely, as Alison Bullock and Hywel Thomas (1997) have demonstrated (see *Table 6.1*). Also, GM schools have been funded at a more generous level than LEA schools to compensate them for the loss of LEA services which they forgo when they become grant maintained.

One might also argue that the historical lower levels of funding for primary-aged pupils are inequitable, particularly since the introduction of the National Curriculum and that resources should be reallocated to provide more equitable funding

Table 6.1: Schools at the centre?

Age	Local Education Authority										71 LEAs Summary stats			Age
	Cleveland	Coventry	Derbyshire	IoW	N. Yorkshire	Redbridge	Somerset	Sunderland	Tameside	Warwickshire	min	mean	max	
3	976	1,252			941	1,258	921	1,108	1,186	789	12	984	1,651	3
4	856	1,064	887	801	861	1,031	921	1,124	1,145	789	704	935	1,285	4
5	856	803	783	801	816	804	921	827	837	789	634	840	1,092	5
6	856	803	783	801	816	804	921	799	837	789	634	831	1,017	6
7	814	795	802	801	792	804	806	799	812	789	614	804	1,025	7
8	814	795	806	869	792	804	806	799	812	789	614	800	935	8
9	814	795	806	869	792	804	806	799	812	789	617	810	987	9
10	814	799	806	869	792	804	806	799	812	789	617	820	1,002	10
11	1,139	1,239	1,135	1,302	1,146	1,272	1,133	1,309	1,170	1,073	869	1,128	1,468	11
12	1,139	1,239	1,135	1,302	1,146	1,272	1,133	1,309	1,170	1,073	869	1,148	1,468	12
13	1,139	1,239	1,135	1,392	1,221	1,272	1,133	1,309	1,170	1,073	913	1,179	1,468	13
14	1,453	1,594	1,381		1,435	1,525	1,484	1,368	1,495	1,436	1,105	1,383	1,633	14
15	1,563	1,732	1,497		1,607	1,525	1,591	1,368	1,609	1,436	1,217	1,475	1,901	15
16	1,917	1,798	1,792	2,325*	1,921#	2,148	1,901	1,664	1,869	1,862	1,428	1,843	2,325	16
17	1,917	1,798	1,803	2,325*	2,062	2,148	1,901	1,664	1,934	1,862	1,501	1,878	2,325	17
18	1,917	1,798	1,803	2,325*	2,062	2,148	1,901		1,934	1,862	0	1,865	2,630	18
19		1,798		2,325*	2,062	2,148			1,934	1,862	0	1,828	2,325	19

* indicates different funding for 'A' Level and non-'A' Level students in the Isle of Wight
  £2,317 for 'A' Level
  £2,331 for GCSE in the 6th Form
# indicates different funding for 16 year olds in North Yorkshire, reflecting the additional costs in respect of exam fees: £1,890 (non-exam) and £1,952 (exam)
(From Bullock and Thomas (1997) Schools at the Centre? A Study of Decentralisation, London: Routledge.)

for primary schools. This has been attempted by some LEAs, but has led to friction between secondary schools and LEAs, and the ever-present threat of opting out makes LEAs wary of challenging the power of secondary school heads and governors. These issues and their implications for decision-making by school management teams will be discussed in more detail in Chapter 7.

What, then, does research show about the impact of the marketization of education on efficiency, economy, effectiveness and equity? A major study by Rosalind Levačić (1995) provides some of the answers to these questions. She studied the impact of LMS on one local authority, which she called 'Barsetshire'. Levačić found that, nationally, spending per pupil on education had declined in the period 1989–1993 in secondary schools, but had risen in primary schools. In both sectors, however, there had been rising pupil–teacher ratios. One explanation is that increased funding had been used to pay for responsibility allowances and for increased pay for heads and deputies. There is also evidence that schools, especially primary schools, are keeping large unspent balances from year to year. In 1996, a survey by the National Association of Schoolmasters/Union of Women Teachers (NAS/UWT) revealed that there was an average underspend per primary pupil of £100, and of £74 per secondary pupil.

This suggests that economy and efficiency in the use of resources is being practised by schools, but begs the questions about effectiveness and equity. According to Simkins (1994) who summarized a number of important issues arising out of early research into the impact of LMS, the nature of schools' responses to LMS depended upon their circumstances (whether they were 'winners' or 'losers' under LMS formulae, or whether post-LMS they experienced rising or falling rolls) and on the managerial approaches of their leaders. He suggested that in schools with shrinking budgets 'efficiency strategies designed to pursue key priorities with fewer resources are increasingly replaced by economy strategies whose main concern is to save money whatever the long-term costs' (p. 19). Simkins (1994) also argues that effectiveness is a 'dynamic and contested concept':

> dynamic, because definitions — whether explicit or implicit — will, for many schools, change over time as governors, managers and classroom teachers attempt to respond to pressures for change arising inside and outside the school; and contested because, for many schools, the various ways in which effectiveness may be defined may not prove easily reconcilable. (p. 25)

Simkins also raises the question of equity in the ways in which schools choose to use their resources. It has been suggested by a number of commentators that the emphasis placed on examination and test results and the publication of league tables will lead schools to be more selective in their admissions policies and to be more likely to exclude pupils who exhibit behavioural problems that might affect the school's image or place heavy demands on teachers' time and other resources. The inexorable rise in the numbers of pupils being excluded from primary and secondary schools seems to indicate that these predictions have proved to be accurate. There has also been a steep rise in the numbers of pupils being given statements of special educational needs, which also indicates that schools are demanding extra resources to help them cope with pupils with difficulties.

Activity

Consider the four 'E's' — Efficiency, Economy, Effectiveness and Equity — and try to answer the following question:

- How far is your school's allocation of resources constrained by considerations of economy rather than efficiency?

- If there is room for manoeuvre, is your school's allocation of resources efficient?

- Is there agreement in your school about what 'effectiveness' means and its relationship to efficiency?

- Is your school pursuing a policy of 'equity'? How can this be demonstrated?

A major body of work about the impact of LMS on schools has been carried out by Stephen Ball and colleagues, who have been researching in a number of schools in London boroughs since the late 1980s. Their book *Markets, Choice and Equity in Education* (Gewirtz, Ball and Bowe, 1995), has, as its title suggests, examined the impact of markets and school choice on the issue of equity. They found that clusters of schools generated a number of different 'markets' and 'choosers'. The markets, they termed 'circuits of schooling', and suggested that there were three of these — and a separate 'circuit' of Catholic schools:

1   A circuit of *local, community, comprehensive schools* which recruit the majority of their students from their immediate locality, have highly localized reputations, and have policies and structures which relate to a comprehensive school identity.

2   A group of *cosmopolitan, high profile, elite maintained* schools which recruit some, or often many, of their students from outside of their immediate locale, that have reputations that extend well beyond their home LEAs, some of which are overtly selective and others of which have 'pseudo-selective' or limited catchment criteria. These schools are usually over-subscribed.

3   A system of *local day, independent schools,* which compete with the maintained sector and which provide alternatives or possibilities for parents who also make a choice within maintained schools.

4   In this study, there was also a fourth parallel, but separate circuit of *Catholic schools* which had its own hierarchy and pattern of competition.

The authors also identified three groups of choosers:

1   *Privileged/skilled choosers,* who are almost exclusively professional middle class and have always been advantaged in terms of their access to educational resources. These choosers are inclined to a consumerist approach to

choice of school, that is, the idea and worth of having a choice between schools is valued and there is a concern to examine what is on offer and to seek out 'the best'.

2   *Semi-skilled choosers* tend to come from a variety of social class back-grounds, but are likely to include working-class families who are strongly motivated to make the most of the opportunities for choice offered by open enrolment. However, they do not have the skills and information networks to maximize their children's advantage. Thus they are often frustrated in their choices and have to settle for local comprehensive schools, although they would prefer the more elite cosmopolitan schools.

3   *Disconnected choosers* are almost exclusively working class. The market is of limited relevance to this group as they tend not to participate in it. They are primarily oriented towards the local comprehensive schools since they have a positive attachment to the locality and going to school with friends and family. Their decisions about schooling for their children are constrained by the demands of work and household organization, low income and lack of transport. They make active and positive choices, but not within the param-eters of the 'consumerist market' in which other parents are operating.

The authors argue that the interaction of the circuits of schooling and the various types of choosers is leading to greater social stratification of schools and to the cumulative advantaging of elite, cosmopolitan maintained schools which are usually over-subscribed, *vis-à-vis* the local community comprehensive schools which may be under-subscribed. Under-subscribed schools will have constrained budgets and may have a student population which is more needy in terms of resources than the elite schools. This makes it extremely difficult for local community comprehen-sive schools to match the perceived quality of service of the cosmopolitan schools.

The case of The Ridings School in Calderdale was an extreme example of how this has worked out in one LEA. *Table 6.2* gives the GCSE results of the 17 schools in the LEA. The circuits of schooling described above can be seen clearly here.

The Ridings School came to public notice because there appeared to be a complete breakdown of order in the school. However, the table shows a number of features that must also raise questions about equity and the role of markets in school choice:

*   The wide discrepancies in achievement between schools — from 91 per cent at Crossley Heath School to 1 per cent at The Ridings School.
*   The fact that, despite a selective system (or perhaps because of it), the percentage of children gaining 5 or more grades A–C in Calderdale was below the national average.
*   The large number of GM schools in the LEA which has drained resources away from the remaining LEA-maintained schools.
*   The fact that choice was not an option for many parents in the more deprived areas of the LEA.

Table 6.2: Highs and lows

1995 GCSE Results in Calderdale. Percentage attaining those grades

		5+ A - C	5+ A - G	1+ A - G
Brighouse High School	GM Comp	43	86	98
The Brooksbank School	GM Comp	44	86	92
Calder High School	LEA Comp	41	80	89
Crossley Heath School	GM Grammar	91	100	100
Halifax Catholic High School	GM Comp	35	80	93
The Halifax High School	LEA Comp	6	59	89
Hipperholme & Lightcliffe High	GM Comp	40	90	94
Hipperholme Grammar	Independent	75	100	100
Holy Trinity CE Senior School	GM Comp	41	98	99
North Halifax Grammar School	GM Selective	83	99	99
Rastrick High School	GM Comp	49	88	93
The Ridings School	LEA Comp	1	40	64
Rishworth School	Independent	61	99	99
Ryburn Valley High School	GM Comp	37	81	94
South Halifax High School	LEA Comp	2	59	79
Sowerby Bridge High School	LEA Comp	23	84	90
Todmorden High School	LEA Comp	28	82	93
LEA Average		37	81	91
England Average		44	86	92

Source: Department for Education and Employment published figures

Activity

See if you can identify the elite and the local comprehensive schools.

Where do you think Sowerby Bridge and Todmorden fit into the pattern?

Now think of the market in which your school operates. Where is your school placed?

Do a SWOT analysis — list your school's Strengths, Weaknesses, Opportunities and Threats in the local market place.

What strategies might this suggest for your school?

The Ridings School had been formed from the amalgamation of two schools in an attempt to cut out surplus places. What such strategies also do, paradoxically, is to reduce choice, for, in order for choice to work, there have to be surplus places. In schools that are over-subscribed, methods for allocating places have to be put in place. There have been accusations of 'covert' selection in the ways in which some schools have done this. Many schools have used interviews with the prospective pupils and their parents and this has been interpreted as schools wishing to choose pupils who will be well-behaved and motivated and have supportive parents. Some former comprehensive schools have put systems of selection according to ability in place. These emphasize more than just academic ability and may focus on ability in music, sport or languages.

What the example of The Ridings makes clear is that if one or two schools are obliged to take the pupils who have been rejected by other schools, a situation of low esteem, low morale and low funding will make it difficult for these schools to perform well.

What alternatives might there be to mitigate the more extreme effects of parental choice?

1   In some areas of the United States where school choice is operating, a lottery system is used to allocate places in over-subscribed schools. All the prospective students, names go into the hat, and are drawn by lot.

2   In the former Inner London Education Authority (ILEA), pupils were classified into three bands according to ability. Each secondary school could take 25 per cent Band 1, 50 per cent Band 2 and 25 per cent Band 3 pupils. This ensured a broadly comprehensive intake into schools. This would be easy to implement on the basis of SAT scores, and would create a level playing field against which schools' effectiveness could be judged.

Activity

Is parental choice the most efficient and fairest way to allocate school places?

If not, what would be a better way?

Does selection improve overall educational standards? If so, on what grounds should pupils be selected?

Should schools take responsibility for modifying the effects of school choice or should they be concerned only with their own survival?

Is collaboration rather than competition between schools a possibility in a market-driven system?

---

3 Secondary schooling could remain comprehensive until the age of 14, and then pupils could opt for a vocational or an academic route at senior secondary school. This system operates in many countries in mainland Europe, along with a presumption that, until 14, children will go to their nearest local school. Thus the choice is made by pupils on the basis of which route they wish to follow.

The situation at The Ridings School appeared to be the result of an extreme form of polarization caused by competition. But, in some areas of the country, schools have found it possible to collaborate in order to mitigate these more extreme effects. Research by Lunt, Evans, Norwich and Wedell (1994), seems to indicate that, for some schools, collaboration is still a possibility. For example, six comprehensive schools in one town have pooled resources to form a behaviour support team, which works in all the schools according to their needs. This has meant that the merry-go-round of expulsions, where pupils with problems are moved from one school to another has been avoided, and schools support each other to support difficult children (see Lunt et al. 1994). In a number of areas, primary schools have formed clusters with their local secondary school to share resources and expertise over a number of areas, including special educational needs. The primary schools are concerned to keep their numbers stable, and not to 'poach' children from each other. The secondary schools welcome the links they have with the primary schools, not least because they hope to recruit the maximum number from them at transfer.

There are many other examples where schools can and do support each other and share resources, for example for INSET and curriculum development work. It is more common in the primary than the secondary sector, but examples can be found at all phases of education (see Macbeth, McCreath and Aitchison, 1995).

Socially Responsible Marketing?

Schools are paying much more attention than they have in the past, to their 'image' and the ways in which they can attract pupils. This involves producing attractive publicity material, having attractive grounds and reception areas, holding open days for prospective parents, getting positive publicity in local newspapers, adopting uniforms for pupils, and so on. Gewirtz et al. (1995) have analysed the image-making that schools have been involved in and the signs and signals (semiotics) that they are adopting. For example, they describe the ways in which schools go to great lengths to have attractive entrances with potted plants and low coffee tables in their waiting areas. One school they visited had a number of clocks on the wall giving the time in New York, Tokyo and Hong Kong!

Apart from these signals to parents, many schools are re-fashioning themselves to present an image that they feel will appeal to middle-class parents. For example, more traditional uniforms (a move away from sweatshirts back to blazers), the display of cups and other honours, and the celebration of high academic results. Whitty, Power and Halpin (1998) have argued that far from becoming more diverse, schools are becoming more alike in their attempts to model themselves on the traditional grammar school.

It has been argued that, in a post-modern world, people find their identity through consumption rather than the work they do. Therefore a choice of school is a 'life-style' choice, and education has become a commodity that people will choose on the basis of image, rather than of substance.

What should be the role of schools in ensuring that the substance of schooling is sound, and that the image does not take precedence? In a thoughtful analysis, Jane Kenway and colleagues have called for 'socially responsible marketing' (Kenway, Bigum and Fitzclarence, 1993). They argue that the distinction between the commercial world and education has become blurred, with schools acting like businesses, and with businesses increasingly trying to market themselves through schools. She cites a number of examples, such as computer vouchers offered by supermarkets, and, in the USA, an educational television channel that also shows advertisements.

Conclusion

Schools and their management teams will have to decide whether their marketing activities are appropriate and whether the commercialization of some aspects of education is justified. Is the role of the school to try to ensure its survival and use all means to do this in competition with other schools in its area? Or do schools have a wider responsibility to their local communities, which will include: the acceptance of pupils with problems and learning difficulties; the maintenance of a balance between academic success and personal growth and development; and the cultivation of a critical awareness of the social and political environment in which they are operating?

References

AUDIT COMMISSION (1985) *Audit Commission Handbook: A Guide to Efficiency, Economy and Effectiveness*, London: Audit Commission.

BULLOCK, A. and THOMAS, H. (1997) *Schools at the Centre? A Study of Decentralisation*, London: Routledge.

CENTRE FOR CONTEMPORARY CULTURAL STUDIES (CCCS) (1981) *Unpopular Education*, London: Hutchinson.

DfE (1992) *Choice and Diversity*, London: HMSO.

DfEE (1997) *Excellence in Schools*, London: The Stationery Office.

GEWIRTZ, S., BALL, S. and BOWE, R. (1995) *Markets, Choice and Equity in Education*, Buckingham: Open University Press.

KENWAY, J., with BIGUM, C. and FITZCLARENCE, L. (1993) 'Marketing education in the post-modern age', *Journal of Education Policy*, **8**, 2, pp. 105–123.

LAWTON, S. (1992) 'Why restructure? An international survey of the roots of reform', *Journal of Education Policy*, **7**, 2, pp. 139–154.

LEE, T. (1996) *The Search for Equity*, Aldershot: Avebury.

LEGRAND, J. and BARTLETT, W. (1993) *Quasi-markets and Social Policy*, London: Macmillan.

LEVAČIĆ, R. (1995) *Local Management of Schools: Analysis and Practice*, Buckingham: Open University Press.

LUNT, I., EVANS, J., NORWICH, B. and WEDELL, K. (1994) *Working Together: Inter-School Collaboration for Special Needs*, London: David Fulton.

MACBETH, A., MCCREATH, D. and AITCHISON, J. (1995) *Collaborate or Compete? Educational Partnerships in a Market Economy*, London: Falmer Press.

PETERS, T. and WATERMAN, R. (1982) *In Search of Excellence: Lessons from America's Best-run Companies*, New York: Harper and Row.

SIMKINS, T. (1994) 'Efficiency, effectiveness and the local management of schools', *Journal of Education Policy*, **9**, 1, pp. 15–33.

TOOLEY, J. (1996) *Education Without the State*, London: Institute of Economic Affairs.

WHITTY, G., POWER, S. and HALPIN, D. (1998) *Devolution and Choice in Education: The School, the State and the Market*, Buckingham: Open University Press.

Chapter 7

Managing Finance and Resources

One of the most significant changes in the role of school management since the Education Reform Act of 1988 has been the management of the school's financial and other resources. Pre-1988, senior management in schools had very little control over budgets, since these were set and administered by the LEA and there was little opportunity to use resources flexibly by viring money from one budget heading to another. Since the introduction of LMS, the control and administration of the school budget has been the sole responsibility of the head and the school's governing body. This chapter will discuss the role of the management team, working with the governors, in making the best use of the school's financial and other resources to achieve the educational aims of the school.

Key issues for managers:

- Who should be involved in decisions about allocating resources in school? What are the respective roles of:
    the governors
    head
    senior management team
    staff?

- Is there a clear understanding among the management team and governors about the way the budget is made up and what it is to be used for?

- Are resource allocation decisions being made as part of the wider development planning process in the school?

- Are systems in place to prevent misuse of the budget?

The Legislative Framework

Local Management of Schools (LMS) was set up by the 1988 Education Reform Act. The detail of the operation of the key component — financial delegation to schools — has been clarified in a number of circulars. A list of the documents which the government issued in the run up to, and during the implementation of LMS and LMSS is contained in an appendix to this chapter.

Some of the key points from Circular 2/94 will be given here to provide a background for the consideration of the management issues they raise. The Circular states the two underlying principles of LMS:

Formula Funding of Schools — Schools must be funded by a formula that is designed to bring about an equitable distribution of resources based on object-ively measured needs rather than historical spending patterns. Each LEA has to devise its own formula, but it must be as simple and clear as possible. In practice, many LEAs constructed formulae which preserved historical patterns of funding — in particular the disparity of funding between primary and sec-ondary schools.

Delegation — There are two aspects to this: (1) the proportion of the total expenditure on schools which is allocated to the schools themselves; and, (2) the freedom given to governing bodies and headteachers to employ their funds according to their assessment of the school's needs and priorities. The under-lying purpose of schemes should be *maximum delegation* of funds from LEAs to schools.

The Formula

The basic rules of the formula must be simple, clear and predictable in their impact so that heads, governors and the community understand how it operates and why it yields the results it does. The formula should reflect objectively measurable needs rather than historical patterns of expenditure. The central determinant of the needs should be the number of pupils in the school weighted for age. Two other factors should be included: special educational needs (pupils with SEN but without state-ments) and costs for small schools in protecting the curriculum. A smaller propor-tion of funding can be allocated on the basis of 'other factors' (e.g. social deprivation). Funding of pupils based in units for SEN attached to mainstream primary or second-ary schools can include a 'place element' (see below).

Special schools and units are funded on the basis of the number of places available for different types of SEN, rather than on actual pupil numbers. In addition a sum can be given for each enrolled pupil. Enhanced funding can be given for outreach work by special school staff who spend some of their time teaching in the mainstream.

Calculating Pupil Numbers

In order to calculate the funding for a school in any one year, most LEAs use a combination of Form 7 and forecast numbers. This causes some problems for schools, since Form 7 data is collected in January and pupil numbers are those forecast for September, whereas the financial year runs from April to March. Also, schools have little control over their income, since it relies primarily on per capita funding, which is in turn reliant on parental choice. In addition, if a pupil is excluded from school, money will be deducted from the budget for that pupil.

If there are drastic changes in pupil numbers, schools are protected to some extent, as the budget cannot change by more than a given percentage in any one year. However, even relatively small changes in income can have quite a significant impact on planning. It is for this reason that many schools are keeping significant amounts of money in reserve (an estimated £580 million overall in 1997), which is, of itself causing problems. There is a view, for example, that this money should be spent for the good of all schools to tackle the huge problem of decaying school buildings.

Activity

How much do you know about your LEA's formula?

Is it 'simple, clear and predictable in its outcomes'?

What are the differences in funding in your LEA between the various Key Stages?

What are the implications of these differentials?

Do you think the principle of maximum delegation has been adopted by your LEA?

What are the strengths and weaknesses of your LEA's approach to formula funding?

What are the implications of the formula for your school's budget?

Salary Costs

The actual costs of teachers' salaries must be charged to schools' budgets but some protection can be made available for small schools. The charging of actual, rather than average, salary costs to schools has been a significant factor in changes to the staffing structure of many schools. There has been a large increase in the use of classroom assistants, particularly in primary schools, so that class sizes have risen, but classroom assistants have been employed to keep the adult to child ratio within acceptable limits, at least for part of each day. The use of classroom assistants raises a number of questions about their training, conditions of employment and responsibilities in the classroom. This is particularly the case when they are employed, as they often are, to work with pupils with special educational needs. One might question why the children who are the most difficult to teach are being dealt with by the least qualified people. Another outcome of the way in which salaries are funded is that older, more experienced, teachers have been encouraged to take early retirement, so that younger, less expensive teachers can be employed. Thus, in the years up to 1997, after which it became more difficult to take early retirement, many experienced teachers were lost to the profession, causing problems with covering shortage subjects, such as maths and foreign languages.

Governing bodies are required to have clear pay policies for all staff — headteachers, main-scale teachers and support staff — which are reviewed annually. As well as rewarding and encouraging good performance, a pay policy must also take into account the need to recruit suitably qualified staff where they are needed. Thus, the pay policy must be part of the overall development planning for the school. This is discussed in more detail below.

Managing the Budget in School

Although this chapter deals mainly with the financial aspects of management, these cannot be seen in isolation from the wider management tasks which LMS has brought to schools. The key areas of LMS as they affect resource management planning are:

1 Financial delegation;
2 Formula funding;
3 Open enrolment;
4 Staffing delegation;
5 Performance indicators.

These are in a *dynamic* relationship. That is, the amount a school receives from formula funding is dependent upon its success in attracting pupils through open enrolment. Financial and staffing delegation are key decision-making areas that will have an impact on the quality of education offered by a school and thus on its attractiveness to parents. The performance indicators, such as SAT scores, GCSE results, exclusion rates and so on, which have to be placed in the public domain, are both an outcome of the way resources are used, and a source of information to parents and to school management. Thus, all these elements of LMS are interacting and have a bearing on planning and decision-making by management and governors.

Before LMS, schools had a restricted *spending* function, and key *resource management* decisions were made by the LEA. Under LMS, the school's traditional *spending* function has to be replaced with a whole-school budgetary process and plan.

The Budgetary Process

> Budgeting has always been perceived as a process for systematically relating the expenditure of funds to the accomplishment of planned objectives. (Schick, 1972, quoted in Simkins and Lancaster, 1987)

Thus it is more than just managing the money, it involves a whole range of more strategic decisions about the aims and objectives of the school. Simkins and Lancaster (1987) summarize the functions of budgets as:

• Planning and forecasting;
• Communicating and co-ordinating;
• Authorizing;
• Motivating;
• Evaluating and controlling.

These functions can be sub-divided as:

Operational Activities	Strategic Activities
Acquisition	Planning
Allocation	Choice
Spending	Choice
Control	Evaluation

Defining Responsibilities

The roles and responsibilities of management, staff and governors are discussed in detail in other chapters of this book. However, as far as financial decision-making is concerned, it is important that these are clearly spelled out. The role of the governing body is to have a *strategic* overview of the school budget and its relationship to the school development plan. The head and senior management are responsible for monitoring day to day spending and ensuring that systems are in place to do this. They are also responsible for preparing spending plans and budgets and presenting these to governors for their consideration.

Approaches to Budgeting

Most of the advice about how to go about constructing a budget for a school is based on the assumption that organizations have clear objectives and resource allocation is organized in a systematic way to facilitate the achievement of those objectives. This, clearly, is the message about budgeting that is conveyed by DfEE, the Audit Commission and other government publications. In their view:

- budgets should relate directly to fulfilling the objectives of the organization;
- they should relate to *outputs* rather than inputs;
- alternatives should be assessed and choices made;
- evaluation against objectives should take place.

It is obviously desirable that such a rational approach is striven after, but ignores many of the realities about decision-making in schools (and in organizations generally). In fact, organizations are highly micropolitical and many decisions are taken because of institutional politics and not because of rational motives. Managers have to judge the extent to which they are able to take rational, strategic decisions (with the support of the governors) and how much account they must take of institutional politics.

> If politics is regarded as conflict over whose preferences are to prevail in the determination of policy, then the budget records the outcome of this struggle. (Wildavsky, 1968, quoted in Simkins and Lancaster, 1987)

There are two approaches to setting a base-line against which each year's expenditure should be set:

1 *Incremental* budgeting in which last year's expenditure provides a base from which to make minor adjustments:

> The largest single determinant of this year's budget is last year's budget. (Wildavsky, 1968, quoted in Simkins and Lancaster, 1987)

This approach has obvious advantages for hard-pressed managers:

- The previous year's budget and level of expenditure is not challenged.
- Attention is given to minor adjustments in the spending pattern or the justification of additional spending.

- There is no attempt to assess the validity of existing spending patterns.
- This provides a predictable and stable organizational environment.
- Very little time is needed to collect information and assess alternatives.

But, as must be obvious, there is no attempt to be developmental in this approach. No strategic overview is obtained and no longer term planning is undertaken. This approach may work in times of stability, but is not suitable in a rapidly changing environment.

2   *Zero-based* or *programme-based* budgeting:

> All expenditure should be justified, not just incremental changes year on year.

Programme-based budgeting or zero-based budgeting both rely on a rational approach to planning and allocating resources. Thus the budget should reflect the agreed aims and objectives of the school and its current priorities. These approaches assume that there is no difficulty in agreeing on objectives in education and translating them into programme goals. They assume there is sufficient time and resources to collect all the information required to make rational choices and they ignore the potentially de-stabilizing effect of having constantly to review and justify budgets.

In reality, for the reasons outlined above, budget decisions will be a compromise between the rational, programme-based approach and the incremental approach. This is sometimes known as *satisficing behaviour*:

> The concept of an acceptable solution, which satisfies the different objectives and goals in an organization may be preferred to the most efficient one on rational grounds.

Activity

Using the checklists below, assess whether your school's approach to budgetary decision-making is rational, political or a mixture of the two.

Rational Approach
1   A clear perception of the choices
2   Data collection and evaluation of alternatives
3   Zero-based approach
4   Choice of alternatives to meet objectives
5   Multi-year time-scale
6   Monitoring and evaluation of efficiency and effectiveness of differing strategies

Political Approach
1   Interest groups are the focus of activity
2   Incremental approach to budgeting
3   Goals seen as ambiguous and contested
4   Decisions emerge after a complex process of bargaining and negotiation
5   Decision-making determined by power of groups and may involve conflict
6   There is evidence of satisficing behaviour

What Is Good Financial Management?

The (1993) Audit Commission/Ofsted publication: *Keeping Your Balance* gives useful practical guidelines to help schools carry out their responsibilities. It sets out twelve key standards for financial administration in schools and provides a checklist for schools to assess their performance. These are summarized below.

1 The responsibility of the governing body, its committees, the headteacher and staff should be clearly defined and the limits of delegated authority established.
2 The budget should reflect the school's prioritized educational objectives, seek to achieve value for money and be subject to regular, effective monitoring.
3 The school should establish sound internal financial controls to ensure the reliability and accuracy of its financial transactions.
4 The school should be adequately insured against exposure to risks.
5 If the school uses computers for administrative purposes, it should be registered under the Data Protection Act, 1994. All data should be protected against loss.
6 The school should ensure that purchasing arrangements achieve the best value for money.
7 There should be sufficient procedures for the administration of personnel matters including the payroll where this applies.
8 Stocks, stores and other assets should be recorded, and adequately safeguarded against loss or theft.
9 All income due to the school should be identified and all collections should be receipted, recorded and banked promptly.
10 The school should properly control the operation of bank accounts and reconcile bank balances with the accounting records.
11 The school should control the use of petty cash.
12 School voluntary funds should be administered as rigorously as public funds.

Activity
The standards listed above vary widely in their focus and strategic importance.

For each standard, can you say:

Who should have day to day responsibility for ensuring that the standard is achieved?

Who should have ultimate responsibility for ensuring that the standard is achieved?

What does this tell you about the current allocation of responsibilities for financial decision-making in your school?

Keeping Your Balance provides a questionnaire for schools to complete to check whether they have systems in place to fulfil the standards. You may wish to obtain this and make use of it. This is reproduced as an Appendix at the end of this chapter.

School Development Planning

A great deal of importance is attached to school development planning. It is one aspect of policy-making for the school which should involve the governors, senior management and staff in a process of taking stock, agreeing on aims and objectives and on setting targets and priorities. Knight (1993) suggests that there are four models of planning which could be adopted:

Model A: The Rational Approach

Following this approach (*Figure 7.1*), the planning cycle would start with an analysis of:

- school and community needs;
- school context;
- educational trends;
- school strengths and weaknesses.

This would enable some strategic goals to be set. Then, the school would move on to consider:

- student, parent and community demands;
- changing pupil needs;
- LEA and national policies.

This would lead to some more concrete objectives and priorities.

The next step would be to formulate some plans for action and to consider what resources would be needed. **It is at this point that the financial implications of the plans and their implications for the school budget should be considered.** Then the plans for the school should be implemented and a review should take place to measure their effectiveness in achieving the agreed goals.

Knight (1993) points out that even though these rational, global planning processes are undertaken by schools, the plans they formulate are often not able to be implemented because of unforeseen changes which impact on the school. For example: a change in government policy, such as cutting class sizes at KS 1 means that schools catering for this age group must make this a priority and may therefore have to forego other plans for development. Or: a sudden fall in enrolment may mean that a school has to divert its planning into regaining the confidence of local parents. Or: a teacher on long-term sick leave may place considerable financial strain on a school, leading to changes in budget priorities. Thus, the environment in which

Figure 7.1: The management process

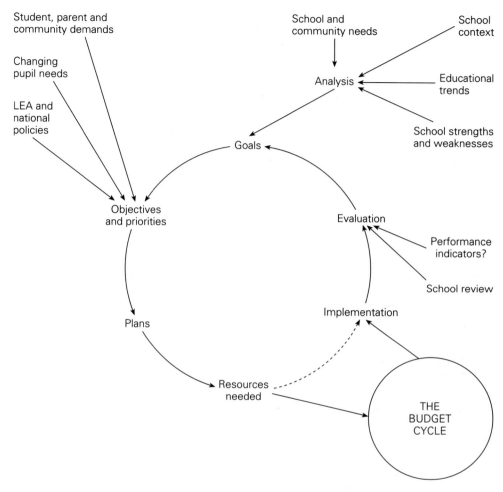

Source: 'The LMS Initiative' Training Package

schools are operating is extremely turbulent, and long-term planning, however desirable, may be inappropriate. This issue is addressed in Chapter 10.

Knight's second model takes account of some of these problems.

Model B: The Pragmatic Approach

This model introduces flexibility into planning by setting objectives but leaving the steps by which to attain them relatively unprescribed. Thus, a goal of increasing levels of attainment may be set, but the specifics of how to achieve this may be left to individual teachers. The danger of this approach, as may be easily seen, is that, without clear plans to achieve a particular goal, things may be left to drift and those who are less committed may more easily opt out. Also, the pragmatic approach may be flexible, but it is essentially a short-term strategy and progress towards the long-term goal could easily lose momentum if the intervening steps and plans of action towards its achievement are not specified.

Model C: The Entrepreneurial Approach

Knight describes this third model as the 'ability to exploit opportunities'. If a school is tied to a prescriptive development plan, or to specific pragmatic objectives, it may ignore opportunities which present themselves, but do not fit into established priorities. For example, links with local business and industry are often set up by taking advantage of one-off opportunities. Some schools have been able to negotiate significant amounts of sponsorship from local and locally-based companies by taking advantage of unplanned opportunities. However, it is important that schools do not get diverted from their core purposes by responding to situations on a whim. This is why it is important to have clear agreed aims, objectives and priorities.

Model D: The Lateral Approach

This fourth approach may involve considering a whole range of solutions to a problem, including those which may appear, at first sight, to be outside the norm. For example, a school might want to think of reducing stress and burn-out in its teachers. One way, not usually considered, might be to completely restructure the school year, having a larger number of shorter terms (maybe four ten-week terms of five eight-week terms) and holidays of differing lengths at different times of the year. Obviously, this would require substantial consultation, and maybe even experiment and evaluation, but there are some schools which are moving in this direction.

In practice, it would appear that school planning tends to be a mixture of rational, pragmatic, entrepreneurial and lateral, and the balance will depend on the management style of the head and governors. Whichever style is dominant, it is important that plans are costed and budgeted for and that clear priorities are set for funding. This means that it is crucial that reliable financial information is made available to the governors to enable them to make decisions on the basis of the resources available to the school. Some examples of effective decision-making by schools are offered in the Ofsted publication: *Managing Financial Resources Effectively in Schools* (Ofsted, 1997).

> **Activity**
> What is the dominant decision-making style of your school?
>
> Using the descriptions given above, identify decisions made using a
> * rational,
> * pragmatic,
> * entrepreneurial,
> * lateral
> style of decision-making.
>
> Evaluate the strengths and weaknesses of each approach and reflect on whether each style was appropriate under the circumstances that prevailed.

Making Budget Decisions

Difficult decisions about priorities often have to be made as the result of financial information. Below is a case-study of a small infant school which had experienced falling rolls and a consequent reduction in its budget.

Figure 7.2: Budget plan

	Allocation	Actual
STAFF		
Teachers	285,492	259,125
Classroom assistants	—	21,988
Early Years CA	16,731	26,987
Supervisory assistants	11,870	15,024
Administration	17,645	15,944
Caretaker and cleaning	13,786	10,176
Clerk to the Governors	—	612
Special Needs	18,693	23,489
	364,217	373,205
Premises	12,330	15,587
Rates	11,360	11,360
Supplies and Services	25,278	22,930
Management Partnership	7,677	7,677
Staff travel	—	750
Training and recruitment	—	500
Real Term Protection	7,681	
Retrospective adjustment (NOR)	6,000	
TOTALS	434,543	432,009
		(2,034)

Parkdale Infants School

The school is a three-form entry infants school in a mainly owner-occupied housing area of a medium-sized town. The standard number is 92, and, until the last two or three years, had been a popular, well-subscribed school. However, in the last two or three years, there had been growing concern among parents about high staff turnover and long-term absence on sick-leave and a perception that standards of teaching and learning in the school were not good. In the previous 15 months there had been a complete turnover of teaching staff (apart from the headteacher) and a number of parents (including three parent-governors) had removed their children from the school. One consequence of this was that instead of an intake of 92 for the coming year, the school has had only 61 applications for places. In addition, the budget for the year from April to March had already been cut because of cutbacks from the LEA. The budget plan for the next financial year is shown in *Figure 7.2*.

There are some interesting variations in this budget between the allocation under the various budget heads and the actual spending in the previous year. Which variations might you wish to question? The staffing arrangements for the school might give you some clues about what decisions have been made. Normally there are nine classes: three Reception, three Year 1 and three Year 2.

Next year, because of falling rolls, there will be eight classes — only two reception classes.

Class sizes will be as follows:

in Year 2   32, 33 and 31
in Year 1   26, 26 and 25
in Reception 32 and 31

Figure 7.3: Staffing structure

	Headteacher (Maths)		

CPS+2	CPS+2	CPS+2	SENCO
Yr 2 co-ordinator (SMT)	Yr 1 co-ordinator (SMT) Science	Early Years Co-ordinator (SMT) English	

Mainscale	Mainscale	Mainscale	Mainscale	Mainscale	Mainscale

NTA*	NTA*	NTA*	NTA*	NTA*	NTA*	NNEB	NTA	NTA	SNA

There are currently nine full-time teachers and a non-teaching head. There is no deputy, but there are three teachers on CPS + 2 who, with the headteacher, make up the senior management team. There is a 0.5 Special Needs Co-ordinator (SENCO) appointment. There are six part-time and three full-time classroom assistants (one specifically for SEN) and 1 full-time NNEB.

The staffing structure is illustrated above (*Figure 7.3*):

The equivalent of the salary of one full-time teacher has been taken from the budget next year.

Activity

The following options could be considered:

1 make one teacher redundant;

2 make the SENCO redundant and employ one teacher half-time to give non-contact time;

3 make the SENCO and 2 full-time classroom assistants redundant (they are on yearly contracts, so do not qualify for redundancy payments);

4 encourage a senior member of staff to take early retirement;

5 cancel plans to refurbish the Early Years section of the school and use some of the school's contingency money to keep staffing at its current level;

6 change back to a head plus deputy management team and give the deputy the SENCO role.

You can, no doubt think of many other alternatives, but what criteria should you use to choose between them?

Whatever the outcome, there are difficult decisions to be made, and these will be made more effectively if linked into the overall planning for the school, which should be set out in the school development plan. In this school, it appears that planning has been incoherent and inconsistent, with no real justification being available for the decisions which have been taken. The school has been under pressure because of poor management and planning, and is now faced with the serious consequences of low staff morale, poor performance academically and falling rolls. In this case, the answer might be to persuade the head to take early retirement and to bring in a new management team and to 'go back to basics' and reconsider the aims and objectives of the school, the staffing structure and deployment of resources and do some thorough auditing of the school's strengths and weaknesses, moving away from incremental decision-making towards a more fundamental review.

Cost-Effectiveness and Schools

One of the key precepts of LMS (and indeed of moves of quasi-markets in many public sector services) is that it should be 'cost-effective' (or as Ofsted put it — 'give value for money'). As many economists have pointed out, it is much more difficult to measure cost-effectiveness in areas such as education than it is in commercial or industrial settings. The Audit Commission suggests that three 'Es' are necessary to evaluate whether public sector services give value for money, as described in Chapter 6: *Economy, Efficiency and Effectiveness*.

Economists give the following definitions of these three terms:

> Economy is the purchase of a given standard of goods or service at the lowest cost;
> Efficiency is the achievement of given outcomes at the least cost;
> Effectiveness is the matching of results with objectives. (Simkins, 1994, p. 16)

Simkins states that there are several types of efficiency: *production* efficiency concerns the relation between resource inputs and outputs. It comprises *technical* efficiency — combining resources in ways which maximize output per given unit of input — and *price* efficiency — choosing that combination of resources which makes best use of a budget given a particular pattern of relative prices. As Simkins argues, particular educational objectives may be achieved in a number of ways, all of which might be technically efficient, but only one of these is likely to be price efficient for any particular pattern of prices. LMS, by allowing virement between budget headings, is clearly designed to make schools more price efficient — i.e. give better 'value for money'.

However, questions of efficiency do not address the question of what should be the outputs that schools are striving for. In schools, these are many and varied, and often the subject of contestation. The government has set targets for the key stages of education, so these are one output which is expected. But parents, teachers and the wider community might have other outputs (or outcomes, which may be longer term) which they wish schools to achieve.

Thomas and Martin (1996) link these economic definitions of efficiency and effectiveness with the educational definitions of 'effective schools' to define a 'cost-effective school' as follows:

> effective schools are those in which pupils of all abilities achieve to their full potential. Whether that performance is achieved using more rather than fewer resources is

not, strictly part of the assessment of effectiveness. On the other hand, the amount of resources is an essential component of the assessment of cost-effectiveness. Thus, if two schools which are comparable in every respect are equally effective in terms of performance, the one that uses the smaller amount of resources is the more cost-effective. A school that uses its resources more cost-effectively, moreover, releases resources which can be used to promote further development. Cost-effectiveness, in this sense of the term, is highly desirable. (Mortimore et al. quoted in Thomas and Martin, 1996, p. 22)

You may wish to reflect to this statement and think of some ways in which an ever-increasing squeeze on costs in schools may eventually lead to effective schools becoming less effective.

Thomas and Martin suggest there are a number of ways in which schools can try to become more cost-effective:

- Periodically undertake a *radical audit* of resources, particularly in the use of staff. Use of premises should be characterized by creativity and diversity. Decisions on resources will differ from the past and the audit of professional development needs must take this into account.
- Improve information on *costs*. Financial information is more likely to be cost-centred. Choices will be assessed in terms of an awareness of foregone opportunities and their costs.
- Use the expertise of relevant staff on resource priorities through some *internal delegation* of decision-making on resources.
- Limit the dangers of complacency about standards and quality by ensuring that the structure of decision-making provides for a *dialogue of accountability* of high quality.
- Reduce the *detachment of management* by using team meetings, appraisal and surveys to collect information on the quality of teaching and learning from teachers, parents and pupils.
- Develop sources of information which are *independent* of head teachers and teachers. (Thomas and Martin, 1996, pp. 42–43)

Schools can compare their use of resources with other similar schools by using the *Benchmarking* materials supplied by the DfEE. These provide a format for groups of similar schools to exchange information about the ways in which they use their budgets.

Conclusion

In order for these levels of efficiency and effectiveness to be achieved, heavy demands will be made of senior management and governors, as well as of staff. Schools will need to be aware of the training and development needs of all the individuals who play a part in the running of schools. Using resources effectively will involve valuing and developing staff, choosing the best quality staff and equipment that the school can afford within its budget and endeavouring to increase the financial and other resources available to the school from sponsorship and community involvement.

Appendix 'Standards' Questionnaire

This list summarizes the Standards and may be of use to schools in monitoring their procedures, and in preparing for audit and inspection visits.

The 'NOT APPROPRIATE' box is used to record a comment if the measure is impracticable, for example owing to a school having few staff. Alternatively the measure might be inappropriate because the school uses a different procedure in accordance with local authority regulations or the DFE requirements of the Rainbow Pack.

1 ORGANISATION OF RESPONSIBILITY AND ACCOUNTABILITY

		IN PLACE	ACTION NEEDED	NOT APPROPRIATE (COMMENT)
1.1	Key roles defined			
1.2	Clear limits of delegated authority			
1.3	Register of pecuniary interests			
1.4	Sound internal control systems			
1.5	Compliance with financial regulations			

2 BUDGETS

		IN PLACE	ACTION NEEDED	NOT APPROPRIATE (COMMENT)
2.1	Statement of aims and objectives			
2.2	Medium term plans			
2.3	Budget planning timetable			
2.4	Timely estimates			
2.5	Planning for solvency			
2.6	Details of budget to LEA or DFE			
2.7	Budget profiling			
2.8	Regular reports to governing body			
2.9	Responsibility of budget holders			
2.10	Regular reviews of budget			
2.11	Virement procedures			
2.12	Monitoring progress against plan			
2.13	Consultation on information quality			
2.14	Reporting proposed policy changes			
2.15	Capital expenditure controls			

3   INTERNAL FINANCIAL CONTROL

		IN PLACE	ACTION NEEDED	NOT APPROPRIATE (COMMENT)
3.1	Duties/checks specified by governors			
3.2	Agreed written procedures			
3.3	Cover for staff absence			
3.4	Separation of duties: records/cash			
3.5	Rules for document alteration			
3.6	Security of accounting records			
3.7	Traceability of transactions			
3.8	Limited access to accounting records			

4   INSURANCE

		IN PLACE	ACTION NEEDED	NOT APPROPRIATE (COMMENT)
4.1	Review of insurance arrangements			
4.2	Reviewing insurance needs			
4.3	Notification of new risks			
4.4	Consent for third party indemnities			
4.5	Notification of insurance claims			
4.6	Insuring property off site			

5   COMPUTER SYSTEMS

		IN PLACE	ACTION NEEDED	NOT APPROPRIATE (COMMENT)
5.1	Data protection registration			
5.2	Back-up procedures			
5.3	Protection of computer facilities			

6   PURCHASING

		IN PLACE	ACTION NEEDED	NOT APPROPRIATE (COMMENT)
Value for money				
6.1	Testing the market			
6.2	Procedures for getting quotations			
6.3	Limits of authority			
6.4	Procedures for accepting quotations			
6.5	Procedure for tendering			

Orders for goods and services

		IN PLACE	ACTION NEEDED	NOT APPROPRIATE (COMMENT)
6.6	Written orders used			
6.7	Official order forms used			
6.8	No private orders			
6.9	Proper completion of order forms			
6.10	Approved certification of orders			
6.11	Responsibilities of signatories			
6.12	Recording committed expenditure			

Payment of accounts

6.13	Checking goods and services received			
6.14	Payment procedures			
6.15	Certification of invoices			
6.16	Authorised signatories			
6.17	Marking invoices 'Paid'			
6.18	Rules for photocopied invoices			

7 PERSONNEL

		IN PLACE	ACTION NEEDED	NOT APPROPRIATE (COMMENT)
7.1	Procedures for personnel matters			
7.2	Procedures for administration			
7.3	Separation of duties			
7.4	Security of personnel records			
7.5	Proper payroll transactions			
7.6	Regular payroll checks			

8 THE SECURITY OF STOCKS AND OTHER PROPERTY

		IN PLACE	ACTION NEEDED	NOT APPROPRIATE (COMMENT)
8.1	Responsibility for cash and property			
8.2	Maintenance of stock levels			
8.3	Maintenance of inventories			
8.4	Checking inventories			

		IN PLACE	ACTION NEEDED	NOT APPROPRIATE (COMMENT)
8.5	Procedures for property off site			
8.6	Authorisation of write-offs and disposals			
8.7	Security of safes and keys			

9 INCOME

		IN PLACE	ACTION NEEDED	NOT APPROPRIATE (COMMENT)
9.1	Governors' charging policy			
9.2	Separation of duties			
9.3	Prompt issue of invoices			
9.4	Issue of official receipts			
9.5	Transfer of money between staff			
9.6	Secure records of income			
9.7	Security of monies			
9.8	Banking arrangements			
9.9	Avoiding unofficial payment			
9.10	Reconciling income and deposit			
9.11	Writing off debts			

10 BANKING ARRANGEMENTS

		IN PLACE	ACTION NEEDED	NOT APPROPRIATE (COMMENT)
10.1	Procedures for cheque book use			
10.2	Regular statements and reconciliations			
10.3	Staff responsibilities			
10.4	Surplus			
10.5	No use of private bank accounts			
10.6	No borrowing			

11 PETTY CASH

		IN PLACE	ACTION NEEDED	NOT APPROPRIATE (COMMENT)
11.1	Agreed level of petty cash			
11.2	Authorised access to petty cash			

		IN PLACE	ACTION NEEDED	NOT APPROPRIATE (COMMENT)
11.3	Clear responsibilities for petty cash			
11.4	Personal cheques not encashed			
11.5	Checks on funds			

12   VOLUNTARY FUNDS

		IN PLACE	ACTION NEEDED	NOT APPROPRIATE (COMMENT)
12.1	Efficient custody and control			

(*Source*: with kind permission of Ofsted)

Key Documents Relating to LMS:

Local Management of Schools. A Report to the DES, (1988) Coopers and Lybrand
Circular 7/88 — Education Reform Act: Local Management of Schools
Circular 7/91 — Local Management of Schools: Further Guidance
Extending Local Management to Special Schools. A Feasibility Study for the DES Touche Ross Management Consultants
Circular 2/94 — Local Management of Schools

References

AUDIT COMMISSION (1993) *Keeping Your Balance: Standards for Financial Administration in Schools*, London: Office for Standards in Education.
KNIGHT, B. (1993) *Financial Management for Schools: The Thinking Manager's Guide*, Oxford: Heinemann.
OfSTED (1997) *Managing Financial Resources Effectively in Schools*, London: The Stationery Office.
SIMKINS, T. and LANCASTER, D. (1987) *Budgeting and Resource Allocation in Educational Institutions*, Sheffield: Sheffield City Polytechnic.
SIMKINS, T. (1994) 'Efficiency, effectiveness and the local management of schools', *Journal of Education Policy*, **9**, 1, pp. 15–33.
THOMAS, H. and MARTIN, H. (1996) *Managing Resources for School Improvement: Creating a Cost-effective School*, London: Routledge.

Chapter 8

Managing across the Boundaries

One of the key tasks of management is managing external relations, that is, acting as the interface between the organization and the 'outside world'. Schools have, until recently, been somewhat 'closed' organizations, relatively unaccountable to parents or their communities, or to society at large. The Conservative reforms of the 1980s and 1990s have made schools more accountable and more permeable to outside influences. Schools must now respond to parents, governors, LEA officers, Ofsted, the local community, local employers and colleges and to the students themselves. This makes the task of management hugely complex, as there are now many stakeholders who have rights and responsibilities *vis-à-vis* schools.

In addition, there is also a range of professionals who come into schools to work with staff to support students and to enhance their learning. These include specialist teachers as well as social workers, psychologists, medical workers, the police and other groups concerned with children and their welfare. Ensuring that these professionals can work effectively with school staff is also a key task for management.

This chapter will look at the various stakeholders in education and discuss how good management can use their involvement to create a more effective and responsive school.

Key issues for managers are:

- how to balance responding to parents' views with ensuring that the educational process is not undermined and that equity is maintained;

- how to work with other professional groups in an effective and mutually supportive way;

- how to work with the governing body to ensure that roles and responsibilities are clearly defined and acted upon;

- how to use the information generated by Ofsted inspections to enhance the work of the school;

- how to make best use of the LEA and other sources of expertise as a resource;

- how to present the school in a positive light to the local community.

> **Activity**
> Make a list of those individuals and groups whom you consider to be stakeholders in your school.
>
> Then list them in:
> 1 order of importance;
> 2 order of influence.
>
> Does this exercise give you any insight into how you should be responding to each of these groups or individuals?

Parents

Parents are seen as a key group to whom schools must respond. The rights and responsibilities of parents are set out in the *Parents' Charter*, published in 1991 and revised in 1994. The first version set out the purpose of the Charter:

> *This Charter* will help you to become a more effective partner in your child's education. As a parent you have important responsibilities. Good schools work better if they have your active support. Your child's education is your concern — and you will want to play your full part at each stage.
>
> The Charter tells you about the Government's new plans for annual written reports on your child's progress; regular reports by independent inspectors on the strengths and weaknesses of your school; published tables so that you can compare the performance of local schools; and independent assessors on panels which hear parents' appeals if they do not get the school they want for their child.
>
> The Charter also sets out your existing rights to information; your right to choose between available schools; the kind of education you can expect and how you can influence it; and your right to be heard if things go wrong.

The clear message from the Charter is that parents will be empowered by being given information and the right to question what goes on in schools. Thus, the primary accountability within schools is to parents and prospective parents.

Parental involvement in schools has two facets: one concerned with the individual relationship of parents with their child's school and the other concerned with the relationship between the school and the parent body. As Ruth Jonathan (1989) has pointed out, individual parents are concerned about their individual children, and what they might want for their child might not be in the best interests of all the children in the school. The task for senior managers is to balance the needs and rights of individuals with those of the school as a whole. There have been some high profile cases where a pupil has been excluded from school and then reinstated after parental appeal and where teachers and other parents have not agreed with the decision to reinstate. Such difficult situations emphasize the need for clear criteria for decision-making which are transparent to all involved and which can be seen to be fair. They also demonstrate the need for skills in communicating with parents and establishing a dialogue with them, both as individuals and as the parent body as a whole. Many schools have systems of communication with parents about policies and practices in school. But how many schools involve parents actively by seeking their views *before* policy decisions are made?

Activity

Below is a list of policy decisions in which parents might be involved. Tick those which you think they should be involved in and put a cross against those which they should not. If you are unsure, put a question mark:

- school uniform;

- discipline and punishments;

- the length of the school day;

- the time of beginning and ending the school day;

- holiday dates;

- methods of teaching;

- curricular issues;

- staff appointments;

- school buildings (e.g. internal decoration, modifications etc.);

- homework policy;

- school meals;

- school trips and educational visits;

- expenditure on equipment;

- health and safety matters.

Also consider the ways in which parents might be consulted — through a policy forum? A questionnaire? Through the parent governors? There are a number of tricky issues to be resolved here, but it is surprising how few schools actually know what the parents think about key areas of a school's operation. It must be acknowledged that it is difficult to develop ways of communicating with parents that 'gives a voice' to all of them. Parents may find it difficult to tune into the professional discourse of schools and may feel disempowered. It is the school's responsibility to enable a dialogue with parents and to 'hear' what parents are telling them. Sometimes parents need to articulate issues that it is uncomfortable for schools to hear. For example, breakdowns in relationships between members of staff and pupils, where the school may automatically wish to defend the stance of the teacher. Parents who have made a positive choice to send their child to a particular school have the expectation that they will be treated as stakeholders, as indeed they are.

If schools are to attract and retain pupils, they will need to be sensitive to what parents want for their children, which, as research shows, is a very complex set of requirements, but may be summed up as 'happiness' (Coldron and Boulton 1991).

Governors

Another aspect of the involvement of parents (and others) in schools, is as governors. Holt and Hinds (1994) have provided a useful perspective on the relationship between governing bodies and schools. They suggest that it should be based on the following 'core values'.

- It is hazardous to make education the province of professionals only.
- It is good to build and exercise powers through people, in this case governors, who derive their authority from acting as responsible citizens.
- Team work is intrinsically better than solo operation.
- Responsibility, authority and accountability belong to the body corporate and not to individuals.
- Feelings matter.
- It is necessary to be explicit about difficulties and conflicts and the processes for handling them.
- Education is about growing and developing, rather than about filling, informing and imbuing.
- Life is more about co-operating than it is about competing. (p. 8)

Many of these principles will be familiar from other chapters of this book, but it is important to emphasize that they apply to dealings with all the stakeholders in education, not just to school staff.

Depending on the size of the school, there will be three or more parents on the governing body. There will also be representatives from the LEA, the local community, teachers and (for Church schools) the diocese. Sallis (1993) has described the need for heads to build partnerships with governors, and the Audit Commission (1995) has published a useful booklet on teamwork between heads and governors called *Lessons in Teamwork.*

The booklet suggests that the most effective governing bodies are those which:

- agree the distinctive roles of the governing body and the headteacher;
- work together as a team, fostering a supportive, yet constructively critical relationship with the headteacher;
- improve their knowledge and experience through regular training;
- develop their awareness of the community served by the school;
- keep themselves informed about standards of teaching and pupil achievement, using comparisons with other schools to put their own school's performance into context.

It provides a series of checklists for governing bodies to assess their effectiveness in working as a team and working with the management of their school.

From a management point of view, it is vital that a clear distinction is made between the roles of the headteacher and that of the governing body. *The School Governors' Guide to the Law*, published annually by the DfEE lists the respective responsibilities of governors and headteachers in the areas of:

- meetings
- curriculum
- religious education and collective worship
- special educational needs
- finance
- staff
- admissions
- equal opportunities
- discipline and attendance
- providing information
- inspection
- health, safety and welfare
- charging for school activities
- school buildings

> The governing body have a general responsibility for seeing that the school is run effectively, . . . so that it provides the best possible education for its pupils. But they are not expected to take detailed decisions about the day to day management of the school — that is the job of the head. A good head will discuss all the main aspects of school life with the governing body and expect them to offer general guidance. (p. 5)

It must be remembered that the governors are lay people, not professionals, and so it will be incumbent on the headteacher to ensure that they are kept well-informed in order for them to play their part effectively. It will be important to negotiate what the division of roles is, and to work with the governors to agree a shared vision for the school.

The Local Education Authority

The relationship between schools and LEAs has changed dramatically since the introduction of LMS. LEAs have had to redefine and renegotiate their role. Riley (1992), in an article about changing role of LEAs, suggests that four different styles of LEA/school relationship have emerged since the reforms of the 1980s and 1990s. These are:

1 The *traditional shire* authority, which is committed to school-based decision-making and sees its essential functions as 'planning, monitoring, and evaluation and the provision of support services'. Members have a tradition of a low level of intervention and the main impetus for policy proposals comes from officers.

2 The *interventionist authority — with egalitarian purposes* is much more heavily influenced by members, usually with political affiliations on the Left. Equality of opportunity is a guiding principle. Such an authority sees itself as guiding and supporting governors.

3   The *interventionist authority* — *the corporate business* operates as a company with the political leadership acting as directors of holding companies. This model's main focus is on the services that the LEA is legally obliged to provide. It has a corporate local authority structure that can identify changing services and priorities and shift resources accordingly. It has a high level of internal delegation, with officers managing their own specific budgets.

4   The fourth model is an emerging one — the *interactive* LEA, which is proactive, seeking to find a new and creative role for itself rather than being buffeted by a sea of legislative changes. The interactive LEA actively encourages local participation and is accountable for the quality of educational experience offered locally.

How schools interact with LEAs will depend, to a large extent, on the style of the LEA. The traditional shire model, will generally leave schools to get on with the job and only intervene if there is a crisis. The more interventionist LEAs will demand more accountability from schools and will offer more opportunities for schools to be involved in policy-making and implementation. However, the more ideologically inclined LEAs will also constrain schools to follow their guiding principles. Thus there is more scope for conflict between schools and LEAs in this model. The interactive LEA will seek to broaden the constituency of schools and to encourage schools to acknowledge the wide range of stakeholders to whom they have to answer. This will make the task management more complex, since schools will have to be much more open to listening to a range of views about their work and their performance.

In the White Paper *Excellence in Schools* (DfEE, 1997a), the Labour government has outlined its vision of the role that LEAs can play in improving standards in schools. Under the heading: 'A new partnership' the White Paper asserts that:

> The leadership function of an LEA is not based on control or direction. It is about winning the trust and respect of schools and championing the value of education in its community, for adults as well as children.

Activity

Which of the models described above best fits your LEA currently?

Is it a model with which your school feels comfortable?

How will a new model of working influence the relationship between your school and the LEA?

What steps can school managers take to ensure that the more interventionist role of the LEA will enhance the work of the school?

So it seems as though LEAs will have no choice but to conform to the new model, as they will have new responsibilities given to them through legislation: to devise an Education Development Plan in consultation with the DfEE and its schools; to provide bench-marking data for schools; to assist schools in setting targets for improvement; to be more involved with individual schools in monitoring performance in between Ofsted inspections. Both LEAs and schools will be under increasing surveillance from central government, with the objective of raising educational standards.

Office for Standards in Education (OfSTED)

Much of the research and anecdotal evidence about Ofsted inspection suggests that it is extremely stressful for staff. Thus, one of the key tasks for management in schools is to ensure that the process is made as positive and well-organized as possible in order to try and minimize stress and allow teachers to give of their best. The detail of how to manage the inspection itself is covered in Chapter 9. The current chapter deals with the role of senior managers in supporting staff and acting as the interface between the staff and the inspectors. Sheila Russell, in her book *Prepared for Inspection* (1996) writes:

> Most research into the effects on schools of OfSTED inspection has revealed the extent of the stress that individual teachers experience. Phrases such as 'being Ofsteded' and 'surviving OfSTED' are testimony to the uncomfortable nature of the exercise. This stress is largely a consequence of the multiplicity of purposes that inspection is designed to serve.

She suggests that teachers see Ofsted inspection as primarily to identify failure, close schools and weed out inadequate teachers. Going back to the Parents' Charter, quoted above, the government's intention seems to have been to provide an independent source of information for parents and other interested members of the public about a school's performance. In its later manifestation, Ofsted appears to see its primary focus on 'Improvement Through Inspection', which is its catch-phrase. Thus, senior managers can set the tone for the inspection by seeing it as an opportunity to review and improve their school's performance rather than as a threat to expose and punish shortcomings.

The Inspectors have a Code of Conduct to which they must adhere, and senior managers should ensure that this is done. The main points of the Code of Conduct are:

- carry out the work with professionalism, integrity and courtesy;
- evaluate the work of the school objectively;
- report honestly and fairly: communicate clearly and frankly;
- act in the best interests of the pupils at the school;
- respect the confidentiality of personal information received during the inspection.

Schools which are well-managed and have robust development plans and high expectations of teachers and pupils will be able to face the prospect of an inspection with more confidence than schools where management is poor and pupils and staff are under-performing. The inspectors will evaluate the quality of management and leadership as well as that of teaching and learning. The inspectors must evaluate and report on:

- how well the governors, headteachers and managers contribute to the education provided by the school and the standards achieved by all of its pupils;
- the extent to which the leadership and management produce an effective school that promotes and sustains improvement in educational standards achieved and the quality of education provided;

- the impact of leadership — not its intentions;
- the quality of leadership — not the style;
- management as a whole, recognizing the crucial influence of the headteacher but taking account of the contributions of governors and staff.

This reinforces the notion that there are many stakeholders and contributors to the life of a school and that the task of managing these is crucial.

Dealing with Ofsted inspectors, then, should be seen as part of the process of evaluation and improvement and the opportunity to work with outside professionals to identify the school's strengths and weaknesses and make plans for the future. In most schools, the Ofsted report will not come as a surprise. Most schools will already be taking steps to improve on areas of weakness and promote their strengths, as research shows (see Earley, Fidler and Ouston 1996).

The Local Community

The notion of a 'community' is commonly used but ill-defined when writing about schools. It could be defined loosely as all those who have a legitimate interest in the life of the school. This may include people living in the vicinity of the school, local businesses, parents of children at the school who live some way away, members of a particular religious group which is served by the school, members of a particular ethnic or racial group which is served by the school, past pupils of the school. With the abandonment of fixed catchment areas, the community served by a school, particularly in an urban area, may be difficult to define. The most useful definition might be:

All those who think that they have a legitimate interest in and commitment to the school.

So, the school community will include all those who work in the school, as well as all those who feel that they have a stake in the school. Community participation makes itself evident by membership of governing bodies and parent-teachers associations, as well as voluntary help in the school and with fund-raising. Fielding (1996) has written very interestingly on the notion of community as applied to schooling. He quotes from Sergiovanni's book *Building Community in Schools* (1994), where he argues that:

to enable good schools to flourish, we need to rebuild community. Community building must become the heart of any school improvement effort. Whatever else is involved . . . it must rest on a foundation of community building.

Experience in the United States has demonstrated that the involvement of communities in schools has enhanced the learning of children and been of benefit to parents and others who have been involved. This is a new way of responding to parents and other community members, which moves away from a 'market' or 'functional' approach to social relationships in schooling towards a more inclusive and deeper involvement. Fielding sees it as an antidote to the fragmentation which characterizes modern mobile societies. It is also implicit in the notions of 'stakeholding' promoted by the Labour Party.

There are two aspects to the question of community involvement in schools — one is: 'How do we make our school into a community?' The other is: 'How do we involve the community in our school?'

Professional Support for the School

As suggested at the beginning of this chapter, there is a wide range of outside professionals who will be involved in some way or another with the work of the school. This includes LEA support professionals, such as educational psychologists and specialist teachers, as well as members of other professions who will have an interest in the well-being of children in school, such as social workers, education welfare officers, doctors and other medical professionals such as speech therapists, clinical psychologists and school nurses. In addition, the police are often involved, either in their role in crime prevention, or in investigating breaches of the law.

> **Activity**
> Make a list of all outside professionals who have visited your school in the last month and for each visit estimate the time they have spent in the school.
>
> Note whether each professional was mainly in contact with pupils (p) or staff (s).
>
> What does this exercise tell you about the amount of contact the school has with outside professionals and how their time is used?

It is often said that contacts between professionals from different disciplines are difficult, for a number of reasons. These include the following factors:

1   *Type of client contact*
    Teachers are with their pupils all day, every day, and therefore see all aspects of their behaviour and functioning in school. Professionals such as social workers and psychologists see children infrequently and for short periods of time. They may also see children in other settings, such as the home, or in an assessment centre. Therefore the different professionals may form different judgments about children which are not always easy to reconcile. It is important to recognize and value the views of outside professionals, but also to expect that the teachers' views are taken into account. Managers in schools need to give the teachers, who are in direct contact with the children being supported, a voice in any discussions about those children.

2   *Cultural differences between professions*
    Part of learning to be a teacher, or a social worker, or a policeman, is a socialization into the values and norms of that profession. Thus every profession has its learned values, standards, knowledge base, techniques and language (or jargon). It follows that there is ample opportunity for misunderstandings to occur between professionals attempting to solve a common problem. One way in which these differences can be minimized, is for

managers in schools to provide opportunities for different professionals to meet the staff as a whole and to discuss their different ways of seeing and doing. For example, workshop activities around familiar problem situations may give the opportunity to see where misunderstandings are occurring.

3   *Structural differences between professional organizations*
    Each professional group which comes into school is organized in a differ-ent way, and has different lines of management and communication. This often leads to problems about whom to contact, what is an equivalence of status and what are the priorities of a particular professional group which might make them more or less easy to invite into school. The introduction of a 'quasi-market' type of organization into the public services means that there are no common routes for contacting services and this makes it more difficult to establish a stable relationship. Managers in schools need to ensure that agreements are set up with the key professional groups that they need to have contact with, so that it is clear who will be asked to come into the school and on what basis. This will help to reduce the uncertainty that the current situation has engendered.

There are also more individualistic factors which may come into play when school staff are interacting with people from other professions. These include such things as: the relative status of the profession (for example, doctors and educational psychologists (EPs) are better paid and often more highly educated than teachers or social workers); gender differences (teaching is predominantly a female profession, and medicine and psychology are not, thus it is likely that doctors and EPs visiting schools are likely to be male, which sets up certain expectations in interactions).

It is also the case that many of the professionals visiting schools are gatekeepers to extra resources or to important decision-making arenas and therefore seen by schools to be in a powerful position.

Activity
Using the list you generated in the exercise on p. 106, decide, for each profes-sional with whom you have contact whether the contact is positive and useful (+) or negative and counter-productive (−).

Then assess whether this is due to structural, cultural or client-contact factors.

How could negative relationships be improved?

How can you build on and enhance positive relationships?

Conclusion

According to Whittington (1983)

> Professionalism is a strategy of job control in which one of the main prizes is the right to define and determine situations within a given sphere of work. People try,

with varying degrees of success, to maximize control of their work and to minimize control of it by others.

Bearing this in mind, managers in schools need to support their staff in carrying out their professional role according to their professional judgment of best practice. They also need to encourage staff to value the contribution that others, both professionals and lay people, can make to the task of educating children.

References

Audit Commission (1995) *Lessons in Teamwork: How School Governing Bodies Can Become More Effective*, London: HMSO.

Coldron, J. and Boulton, P. (1991) '"Happiness" as a criterion of parents' choice of school', *Journal of Education Policy*, **6**, 2, pp. 169–178.

DfE (1991, 1994) *The Parents' Charter*, London: HMSO.

DfEE (1997) *A Guide to the Law for School Governors*, London: HMSO.

DfEE (1997a) *Excellence in Schools*, White Paper, London: HMSO.

Earley, P., Fidler, B. and Ouston, J. (Eds) (1996) *Improvement Through Inspection?: Complementary Approaches to School Development*, London: David Fulton.

Fielding, M. (1996) 'Beyond collaboration: On the imporance of community', Chapter 13 in Bridges, D. and Husbands, C. (Eds) *Consorting and Collaborating in the Education Market Place*, London: Falmer Press.

Holt, A. and Hinds, T. (1994) *The New School Governor: Realising the Authority in the Head and the Governing Body*, London: Kogan Page.

Jonathan, R. (1989) 'Choice and control in education: Parental rights, individual liberties and social justice', *British Journal of Education Studies*, **27**, 4, pp. 321–338.

Lowe, C. (1992) *The School Governor's Legal Guide* (4th ed), Kingston upon Thames: Croner Publications Limited.

Riley, K. (1992) 'The changing framework and purposes of education authorities', *Research Papers in Education*, **7**, 1, pp. 3–25.

Russell, S. (1996) *Prepared for Inspection: A Practical Guide to Ofsted Inspections*, Westley, Suffolk: Courseware Publications.

Sallis, J. (1993) *Basics for School Governors*, Stafford: Network Educational Press.

Sergiovanni, T. (1994) *Building Community in Schools*, San Franciso: Jossey Bass.

Whittington, C. (1983) 'Social work in the welfare network: Negotiating daily practice', *British Journal of Social Work*, **13**, pp. 265–286.

Chapter 9

Curriculum Management

This chapter attempts to help teachers and managers at all phases and levels of responsibility to find answers to the key questions below. So, rather than address subject-specific considerations, it examines the principles underpinning them. Hopefully, therefore, a maths co-ordinator in a primary school will find it as helpful and thought-provoking as a head of a drama department in a secondary school. There are many more common cross-phase curriculum management issues than there are differences, and these are the ones to be explored here.

Key issues for managers:

- What does 'curriculum' mean and who has management responsibility for it?

- What guides or drives the curriculum of a school?

- How does a well-organized school plan the curriculum and then ensure that its plans are realized?

- Do different teachers and managers have different levels of responsibility for the planning and delivery of the curriculum?

- How can teachers 'manage' an Ofsted inspection?

- What principles should underpin monitoring and evaluating curriculum delivery?

What Do Educators Mean by 'Curriculum'?

The introduction of the Education Reform Act in 1988 focused some educationalists' definitions of 'curriculum' much more clearly (and often with regrets) than before. It often seems now as if educational writers are lamenting for freedoms that have been lost. For example, Brian Fidler (1996, p. 11) writes that 'the school is not free to offer its own curriculum, which reduces the extent to which a school can make itself distinctive'. He sees the curriculum as one of the main instruments which might have distinguished one school from another, as if those professionals with responsibility for the learning and teaching in a school had absolute choices about what constituted the curriculum taught there. But teachers never really did have absolute freedom to choose the curriculum they were to teach: two decades earlier, sociologists of education such as Michael Young (1971) were explaining that those in positions of power are responsible for the assumptions that underlie the selection and organization of knowledge in society — the curriculum. He wrote:

> Education is . . . a selection and organization from the available knowledge at a particular time which involves conscious or unconscious choices. It would seem that it is or should be the central task of the sociology of education to relate these principles of selection and organization that underlie curricula to their institutional and inter-actional setting in schools and classrooms and to the wider social structure. (p. 24)

In recognition of this work, schools and teachers in the 1970s and 1980s began to pay attention to more than the aspects of the curriculum which were organized into traditional subjects. They discussed the social and political construction of sub-jects, and also attempted to define 'curriculum' more carefully. Whitty (1985, p. 40), for example, described American work on 'the overt curriculum, the hidden curriculum and the curriculum-in-use' where writers were trying to read the messages trans-mitted by the curriculum, and to understand why certain messages were transmitted rather than others. Teachers also began to question the learning and values being transmitted within schools other than through the formal curriculum: for instance, issues of race, class and gender were recognized within the order that students were registered and it was agreed that the attention paid to the correct pronunciation of names taught important lessons to everyone listening.

For a short time after the introduction of the Education Reform Act of 1988, the previously broader definitions of 'curriculum' which were encouraged by readings in the sociology of education, seemed in some schools to become narrowed to mean the learning and testing defined by the National Curriculum. Teachers were so overwhelmed by the demands of planning and implementing the National Curriculum (and then changing it all again in some subjects) that they had little time left over to plan for the 'rest of the learning' that takes place in schools. Even so, attempts to keep to the broader definitions could still be seen in the works of various writers. Bowe and Ball with Gold (1992) wrote that as a result of their research in schools during the years after the initial implementation of the Education Reform Act, they found that:

> The National Curriculum, as it stands, is fixed, heavily prescribed and rests on a strongly normative model of progress in learning. The system of national testing carries with it a presupposition of classroom, institutional and area comparisons . . . The National Curriculum provides a potential for a language of hierarchy and comparison based on levels of achievement. Against this the teacher must provide flexibility, differential pacing, individual classroom support, encouragement and reinforcement. But if problems arise what will be blamed first — the teacher or the National Curriculum? (p. 126)

They were attempting to look wider than the National Curriculum when they re-ferred to the multiplicity of the tasks of the teacher. They also make links with Young's ideas when they quote Ken Jones (1979), pointing out that the National Curriculum is a particular selection from national culture.

The Dearing Report (1994) eased the prescriptiveness of the 1988 Act, and gave teachers more time during the school day to teach what they and the rest of those people responsible for planning learning thought they ought to be teaching — teachers interpreted this committee's report as a step towards a recognition of their professionalism, and the return of some of their professional autonomy. In 1998 primary school teachers were told to relax the National Curriculum in order to spend one hour each day on both numeracy and literacy with their classes.

So far in this chapter, a historical tracing of writings about the curriculum has been presented, but still no clear definition of 'curriculum'. Ted Wragg (1997) offers one which takes account of writings by educational sociologists, but also leads us into the twenty-first century:

> I shall take the term 'curriculum' to comprise most of what children learn in school, including what is sometimes called the 'hidden curriculum', that is, the values and patterns of behaviour that are acquired, often incidentally — for example, if pupils learn to show concern for others, or to accept authority. I should not want such an elastic definition to be stretched to include absolutely everything that happens within the boundaries of a school, though others might see it this broadly. If the concept of curriculum were to be that vast and comprehensive, then every single private exchange between pupils, whether reprehensible or not, including those that took place out of sight and earshot of teachers, would have to be called part of the 'curriculum'. In this book 'curriculum' includes what is actively sponsored, or else condoned, by the school and its teachers, whether it is labelled on the timetable or not. (p. 1)

This is the definition that is to be adopted for this chapter — the key words are 'actively sponsored, or else condoned'. They bring with them some idea of the discussion and planning that are necessary when thinking about the curriculum in a school and then the sense of purpose and instrumentality necessary to ensure the direction is followed. Thoughtful teachers and managers come to an understanding, first of the moral dimensions about what is happening in a school, and then they develop clear aims about what should be happening and how to get there.

Before reading the rest of this chapter, it might be illuminating and helpful to complete the following task with a group of your colleagues (or alone):

Activity

Defining 'curriculum'

1   With a group of colleagues or alone, brainstorm 'curriculum', remembering that a brainstorm includes all 'off the wall' ideas, without judgment. The brainstorm should include *any* connections with the word under examination, no matter how tenuous they might seem.

2   When the brainstorm has run out of steam, reflect on the different suggestions, putting a ring round those for which you are able to take direct responsibility.

3   Try to assign those suggestions for which *you* clearly have no responsibility to other members of staff, perhaps by using another colour, thus ensuring that these issues are not forgotten.

4   Keep this brainstorm to refer to when you plan the curriculum more formally within your team. Tick off the suggestions you have ringed as you incorporate them in your planning.

This exercise may serve to broaden the definition of curriculum, to agree how to plan for the delivery of the wider definition, and then to monitor that as many as possible of the components of the definition are taking place in the school.

Who Has Management Responsibility for the Curriculum?

Within Ted Wragg's definition of the curriculum, it becomes clear that *all* teachers in a school (and the governors and other staff without teaching responsibility) either sponsor or condone the learning. He has a democratic view of education, and wishes to encourage all teachers and stakeholders in a school to inform and be informed by that which is sponsored or condoned by the school. So how are they encouraged to acknowledge and plan for this responsibility? How are they given a voice? Where is the forum for this discussion? It is clear that the above questions do not always have the same set of answers in every school. Those people with management responsibility in schools make such choices influenced by their educational philosophy about the extent to which they involve their colleagues in the decision-making, planning and delivering of the curriculum. Some operate as democratically as Ted Wragg suggests, and others work more hierarchically. The Audit Commission (1991) reports:

> Although final decisions on a school's development plan rest with the governing body, the headteacher will take the lead in the preparation of the plan. The headteacher should involve all the staff who will implement it in order to maximise their commitment to its success. (p. 20)

But these management decisions are not as simple as they might first seem: for example, school development planning is one activity that many educationalists suggest allows all school staff a voice in the curriculum of the school. However, Hargreaves and Hopkins (1994) warn that school development planning is not value free, and that involving all the staff of a school in the development plan is not necessarily the democratic activity many people think it may be:

> Teacher participation in school development planning is sometimes portrayed as not only valuable but an appropriate form of organizational behaviour in a democratic society . . . It is instead the arena for the struggle between competing power groups. These arguments are a far cry from any idea that the processes (not content) of school development planning can be seen as outside or immune from value and power laden positions as is sometimes suggested in portrayals of collegial development. (p. 97)

This excerpt from Hargreaves and Hopkins (1994) is not quoted as a critique of school development planning, but to show how difficult it is to give stakeholders real and equal voices in decision-making in a school. Hargreaves and Hopkins go on to quote Stephen Ball (1992) arguing that such ideas as school development planning are not always entirely benign:

> Ideas such as the self-managing school, the developing school or the learning school are from a Mary Poppins 'value free world of consensus, collaboration and self-control' . . . They can be used to ease the acceptance of an overt imposition of management based on a culture of market and budget rather than professionalism . . .

He captures this vividly with the image that the self-managing spoonful of sugar which helps the managerial medicine go down. (pp. 97–98)

There is further discussion about school development plans in the next section. In the meantime, it is necessary to recognize that this account of the impossibility of true democracy in schools is partly explained by an understanding of the micropolitical aspects of power and influence. Those who lead schools often find it almost impossible to cling to their own values and beliefs about education while they are bombarded with the demands of the market place and the constraints of the budget. Their ideas are mediated and influenced by external and internal requirements. And in turn, they work to persuade and influence different stakeholders so that they, too, easily lose sight of their original educational goals, or change them almost imperceptibly to match those prevailing in the school. So, although all adults connected with a school have some responsibility for the school curriculum, those with management responsibility in a school have an added responsibility for encouraging the shared articulation between their colleagues. The warning here is that those with management responsibility need to have a clearer awareness of whether they are encouraging, influencing or allowing that articulation.

Managing an Ofsted Inspection

Managing the paperwork is a key issue for school managers involved in the Ofsted process. When talking to teachers on our courses, it became clear that those who work in schools where there are effective and useful paperwork systems already in place as an integral part of managing the school have found preparation for inspection less onerous and traumatic. It is clear that on the whole, the questions asked and the paperwork demanded by Ofsted teams are those which underpin good curriculum planning practice.

Many experienced headteachers and senior managers in schools, when talking about their experiences of 'being Ofsteded', advise staff in schools which are to be inspected to develop a sense of ownership about the process, in order to understand fully the procedure, but also so that there is some room for negotiation during the actual process. In this way, they see the process as becoming more two-way, and so they hope to have more influence on the outcomes and on the judgments made about their schools.

Here is a summary of some points about the Ofsted procedure:

- Although the main changes in the inspection procedure began in the early 1990s, educationalists took some time to 'read' and make sense of what was happening. In other words, definitions of and research about the effects of Ofsted inspections were really only beginning to be published in the late 1990s. This meant that there was and still is a sense of the unknown about the procedure which has lent it an air of mystery and some fear. (Especially when it became linked with the nomination of good and bad teachers).

- There are very specific management issues about information within the process — it is important to involve the whole staff in the process so that they know what is happening, without overburdening them with unnecessary paperwork.

- If the paperwork that a subject team regularly completes is agreed to be worthwhile by everyone in the team, and is seen as an effective way of monitoring the curriculum in the subject area, it is likely that the team will not have to do large amounts of extra paperwork for the inspection.

- All staff must know and understand where the *Framework for Inspection* impacts on their specific subject area, but at the same time team leaders must try to keep a wider perspective on all their curriculum responsibilities.

Planning the Curriculum — School Development Planning?

The question mark at the end of the phrase above is in order to reflect the changes in name and description of the planning processes which drive a school. Some school managers and governors have action plans, some have school development plans, and others are involved in strategic planning. It is possible to trace an evolutionary line leading through these different ways of organizing the learning and teaching in a school. For some schools the links are mainly historical and contextual, and for others they depend on the level of maturity of the existing planning in the school (and even of the imminence of an Ofsted inspection).

Before 1988, the most successful schools in Britain had well-tried and individualistic systems for reviewing themselves and implementing their priorities. These were usually developed and managed by the Senior Management Team, and they embraced the management of the curriculum linked in with the academic and financial year(s), and including staff development as well as general monitoring and evaluation. By 1988, the Department of Education and Science had given local education authorities (Circular 7/88) the responsibility for ensuring that all schools had School Development Plans in order to give them more responsibility for their own planning. Corrie Giles (1997) writes:

> The literature produced by the DES, LEAs and academics in support of the SDP approach to site-based planning typically portrayed SDPs as a means of helping schools to manage change. In particular, it was considered that the SDP was a useful means of bringing together the medium-term planning priorities of the school and that, although reflecting national LEA and school policies, it could also be used to identify and implement a limited number of whole-school improvements and developments. (p. 3)

Brian Fidler (1996, p. 131) explains the conceptual differences between school development planning and strategic planning. He writes that compared to school development planning, strategic planning is:

- *Forward-looking*: environmental scanning tries to spot future influences.

- *Outward looking*: data are collected from parents and others; the consequences of the school's actions on others are considered.

- *Proactive*: the school is regarded as an initiator — recognizing opportunities and taking advantage of them; reviewing possible impositions from outside and taking a stance on them rather than acquiescing.

- *Creative*: vision is a creative element to balance improvement which would otherwise be based on analysing and improving present practices rather than doing something radically different.

- *Holistic*: it deals with all the school's operations rather than mainly being concerned with schooling and staffing; it also tries to view the school's operations holistically. (pp. 131–132)

The model he is using here for school development planning comes from DES material published in 1989 and 1991: *Planning for School Development* and *Development Planning — A Practical Guide*. Most schools used these publications as a guideline, but those who were committed to serious planning anyway added some of the components of Fidler's strategic planning.

The least long-term and most reactive planning strategy is action planning. This is most common when, after inspecting a school, Ofsted inspectors make a report which includes some key points for action to be addressed. The headteacher and governors are required to make an action plan within 40 days of the inspection to show how they will address the key points. Some action plans become school development plans for the following year, sometimes they are incorporated into the school development plan, and in some schools, most of the key points are already known to the school management, and are already planned for within the school development plan.

These questions (right) introduce another difficult aspect of planning: for review to be effective, it must be possible to change or adapt plans which have become inappropriate, without losing direction or momentum. One of the main criticisms of development planning is that initially when schools attempted to draw up formal five and three year plans in detail, external change made it impossible to keep to the plans and so the management team (and other members of the school) often felt as though they had wasted time, or indeed had failed in their planning objectives. So one of the most important management tasks in planning is to be able to develop plans which help to guide a school and all who work in and around it in an agreed direction, but which are organic enough to be reviewed and adapted where necessary without leaving the stakeholders directionless, in a hiatus or in a planning blight. Chapter 10 takes this discussion further.

Activity

Think about the planning strategy which guides the school with which you are connected. Attempt to answer the following questions about the planning, the school, and your part in the planning:

- Does your school have a school development plan, a strategic plan, an action plan or something else?
- What was your involvement in the formulation of the plan?
- Do you have easy access to the final plan?
- Do you have your own copy?
- To your knowledge, how often is the plan reviewed, and who reviews it?
- Does it change a great deal at each review?
- What are the staffroom reactions when 'development planning' appears on an agenda?

What Guides or Drives the Curriculum of a School?

Most of the literature on school management refers at some stage to the school mission statement, or the vision, or the educational philosophy or the underlying principles of education. Whatever it is called within each institution, it is at the foundation of all education within each school. When managed successfully, it underpins but is visible in every transaction and activity in and around the school. Articulating and sharing a vision is a highly motivating activity for each school community, but this activity easily becomes mistrusted and viewed cynically if it is not directed into action. This section will begin with a definition of 'vision', and then discuss the possibilities of translating the underlying values of an organization through curriculum planning into all activities planned for by the teacher in the classroom. In this way, the vision becomes alive, and the learning and teaching in a school has an agreed direction and an ethical underpinning. Roland Barth (1990, p. 179) wrote:

> Expansion of vision within the schoolhouse is an enterprise that will bring about the kinds of schools in which there is room for all of us to live and work and have our children learn. When we create schools we value for our children and ourselves, we will have created schools of value to others as well.

Wragg (1997, pp. 1–2) lists four propositions for the curriculum, which appear to contribute to *his* vision of education:

1   education must incorporate a vision of the future;
2   there are escalating demands on citizens;
3   children's learning must be inspired by several influences;
4   it is essential to see the curriculum as much more than a mere collection of subjects and syllabuses.

Per Dalin (1993, p. 134) writes:

> Above all, we need school leaders who have a *vision* for their school, that is shaped and developed in close co-operation with staff, students and parents. A school leader is needed to give birth to the vision, to facilitate the process towards this vision and to be a 'backup' whenever needed. A learning organization having a leader who has a sense of personal commitment and mission is well served.

One way of understanding the importance of having a vision for education is to complete the following activity. You might do it by yourself, with a group of colleagues, or in one of the teams in which you work.

When we do this activity with groups of teachers on management courses, they begin it with slight embarrassment, but gradually they become absorbed by it, and finally end up excited and motivated by it. And so members of a school, when completing this activity together, are excited and motivated by it. They quickly become cynical, however, if the activity stops at this point. The clear management task, and the main ethical task, is to find ways of ensuring that members of a school agree a core purpose for the school, and that the core purpose gives strength and support to all curriculum planning in the school.

Activity

1 Think about why you came to work in education. There will be many different reasons and influences, probably reaching far back over your lifetime. Spend some time reflecting on all the reasons.
2 Now, think about your present beliefs and understandings about education, learning and teaching. Why are you still 'doing' it?
3 What do you want for the young people you teach? In not more than two sentences, frame what for you is the core purpose of education.
4 If you are working with other people, at this point, you might like to work in pairs to discuss each person's two sentences.

How Does a Well-Organized School Plan the Curriculum?

Most schools have curriculum leaders (called heads of department in secondary schools) whose responsibility it is to make sure that coherent work is planned within their curriculum area. Usually, it is recognized that this work is best done by teams of people who work within that area, and it is understood that the planning activity is excellent professional development for all concerned. It is also important to make sure that planning in different subject areas is underpinned by the core purpose of the school.

The following activity is one to which we introduce all middle managers on courses with us. You might wish to read it through and even complete it as an example of a way of turning rhetoric into reality.

Activity

You may find that this activity is best completed by a whole curriculum area team, maybe during a staff development session. It is not really necessary that all concerned are teaching the same subject — as long as they are in the same school.

1 In two sentences and by yourself, without referring to any school literature at this stage, sum up the core purpose of your organization (i.e. the basic philosophy of the school). (**This might take about 10 mins**)
2 Check with someone that the sentences make sense. (**Allow about 5 mins each**)
3 Write each set of sentences on a piece of flipchart paper, and post them around the room. (**5 mins**)
4 Walk around and look at all the sentences. What do they have in common? What are the similarities? How might these ideas be connected with ideas about curriculum? (**15 mins**)
5 Flipchart a brainstorm of what constitutes the 'Curriculum' (overt, hidden, received, intended, methodology, pastoral, PSHE, etc.). (**5 mins**)
6 Now attempt to come to an agreement as a group on two sentences to summarize the core purpose of the school. Write the agreed sentences on a sheet of flipchart paper, and post them up. (**15 mins**)

7 Write up to six principles which underlie the *overall curriculum* of your organization — those six principles should relate to the core purpose of your school. (**15 mins if working alone, 30 mins as a group**)

8 Check that the two original sentences and the six principles make sense. Ask the following questions:
Are they congruent?
Do they fit?
Do the sentences lead into the principles? (**10–20 mins**)

9 After checking, copy your 'principles' on to a piece of flipchart paper, and pin it up underneath your sentences of core purpose. (**5 mins**)

10 Establish up to six **basic** principles which (should) underlly *your particular curriculum responsibility*. Write them on a sheet of A4 paper. (**20 mins if alone, 35 mins if working with a group**)

11 Check that those curriculum principles match your organizational principles.

You will probably find that this is a very tiring activity, because it combines quite emotional demands with very practical and organized ones. However, it is highly productive, and leads a team to the point where it can begin to focus on the practicalities of specific curriculum responsibilities. The next part of the activity is to be done with people who work in the same subject area. Before embarking on it, it might be wise to make sure that everyone understands the same thing when the following terms are used:

- curriculum aims/principles
- objectives
- targets — short-, medium- and long-term
- success criteria

In other words, it may be advisable to agree on the terms communally before embarking on the next stage of the activity.

Activity
This work is best done in small groups of about three people who are concerned with learning and teaching in the same subject.

Each person should take one curricular aim/principle from the six departmental principles drawn up previously. Take it in turns to put it into context for the rest of the group.

The group should look at the principle/aim, and:
– frame not more than three objectives to achieve that aim;
– set short-, medium-, and long-term targets for one objective;
– and establish the success criteria for that objective.

Repeat this process for each member of the group. Divide the time between each person equally so that everyone will have a chance to present a curricular aim/ principle.

If this process has not been followed through so logically before, you will probably find that the first time a departmental aim is translated into specific objectives, targets and success criteria, it takes so long that it seems to be an interminable procedure. But subsequently, it becomes much faster, and eventually automatic. That is when the whole activity is really helpful and productive, and all the links connect the school's aims with what actually happens in the classroom. The targets and success criteria set the groundwork for the monitoring and evaluation of the curriculum within this subject area. And the paperwork that comes out of this activity will serve as basic and important documentation for the curriculum area, and also as records for inspection.

Different Responsibilities for Planning and Delivering the Curriculum

The suggestions within this section depend on the organization of a school. Although the senior management team and the governors of a school have ultimate overall management responsibility for the planning and delivering of the curriculum, class or subject teachers have daily responsibility. Most schools are now organized into middle and senior management, and those teachers who are middle managers usually have responsibility to lead the planning.

It is helpful to note that although senior managers have ultimate management responsibility for the learning and teaching in the school, they often do not have the relevant up-to-date knowledge to lead the planning; curriculum leaders are usually more knowledgeable about the daily delivery of specific curricula. It may also be that although curriculum leaders lead the planning, other members of the team divide the responsibility for different parts of the school and different learning stages between them. Linkages between the stages then become very important and there is a need for careful documentation. It is this documentation that allows the curriculum area to present itself well to the rest of the school and other interested people, and the care with which it is designed and operated makes for easy and long-term use with only minor regular review and changes.

There is currently much discussion both outside and inside the teaching profession about the ways the National Curriculum is delivered. There are also discussions about who should monitor what happens in classrooms. In some primary schools, curriculum co-ordinators are appointed to their posts after only a year or two of teaching, and they naturally find it difficult to comment on the classroom practice of colleagues who have been teaching for many years. In these schools, senior managers often decide that classroom practice is a whole-school issue — they draw up policies for all the teaching staff about work in classrooms, and monitor those policies themselves. In secondary schools which are both larger and more hierarchical, heads of department have usually been promoted after several years' experience working in their subject area, and so are more at ease when developing ways of monitoring the teaching and learning within their subject responsibility.

Monitoring and Evaluating Curriculum Delivery

Some teachers believe that the only way a manager can *really* know how the other members of the staff teach the agreed curriculum is by entering their classrooms.

There are several other indicators, and a perceptive manager pays attention to all possible indicators in order to know that good work is going on. These may include:

- discussions about teaching methods;
- sharing materials;
- looking over lesson plans;
- reviewing attainment targets;
- collaborative planning sessions;
- and team teaching.

An agreed formal visit to a classroom while a lesson is taking place, flanked by discussions with the teacher before and after the visit, could be a very productive way for both adults concerned. But classroom observation is a complicated issue, and should not be undertaken lightly.

Beginning teachers and newly qualified teachers are used to classroom visitors, but some long-established teachers still have conflicting and complicated views about their 'privacy' when teaching in their own classroom. The National Curriculum and the Ofsted procedure have made it essential that there should be discussions in schools about the actual activity of teaching. Indeed, DfEE accredited courses for primary curriculum co-ordinators are required to include some time spent on either classroom observation or other ways of ascertaining what is going on in the classroom with reference to co-ordinators' curriculum responsibility.

As probable appraisers of members of staff, managers will be aware that the appraisal process includes a carefully set up classroom observation, in which negotiation about the actual activity to be observed depends on an equal balance of power between the appraiser and the appraisee. Basic understandings about power and equity should be remembered whenever a classroom visit is planned. Formal classroom observation that is a clear and agreed activity by everyone involved, might make teachers nervous and uncomfortable. But, when it is properly done, there will be no hidden agendas. Many managers recommend informal visits, some-times on other pretexts, to see what is really going on in the classroom. Informal visits are easier and less nerve-racking for teachers, but they can be complicated by hidden agendas. Teachers may be given mixed messages: 'I am just dropping in informally, BUT, I am making judgments about your work without proper discus-sion with you'. If members of a departmental team regularly enter each others' classrooms while teaching is going on, and regularly talk about their work together, and if they have an atmosphere of trust and expectations of the best from each other, then informal visits cannot be misinterpreted. But if a team leader's 'drop-in session' is really a way of monitoring teaching without admitting to it, it will be almost impossible to use the evidence gathered, in a helpful and constructive way.

Conclusion

However well-organized a curriculum area is, and however devolved the responsib-ility for monitoring all aspects of it, it is a manager's chief responsibility to raise the consciousness of other members of the team about the definition of 'curriculum'. The width and depth of the curriculum contains within it the educational vision of the school. The connections will be clear and strong in a well-organized school, and will be clearly contributed to by all concerned.

References

Audit Commission (1991) *The Management of Primary Schools*, London: Audit Commission.

Ball, S.J. (1992) 'The worst of three worlds: Policy, power relations and teachers' work'. Paper given at the British Educational Management and Administration Society Research Conference, Nottingham, April 1992.

Barth, R. (1990) *Improving Schools from Within*, San Francisco: Jossey-Bass.

Bowe, R. and Ball, S. with Gold, A. (1992) *Reforming Education and Changing Schools*, London: Routledge.

Dalin, P. (1993) *Changing the School Culture*, London: Cassell.

The Dearing Report (1994) *The National Curriculum and Its Assessment*, House of Commons Education Committee.

Department of Education and Science (1988) *Local Management of Schools*, Circular 7/88, London: DES.

Department of Education and Science (1989) *Planning for School Development*, London: DES.

Department of Education and Science (1991) *Development Planning — A Practical Guide*, London: DES.

Fidler, B. (1996) *Strategic Planning for School Improvement*, London: Pitman Publishing.

Giles, C. (1997) *School Development Planning*, Plymouth: Northcote House Publishers Ltd.

Hargreaves, D. and Hopkins, D. (1994) (Eds) *Development Planning for School Improvement*, London: Cassell.

Jones, K. (1979) *Right Turn*, London: Radius.

Wragg, E.C. (1997) *The Cubic Curriculum*, London: Routledge.

Whitty, G. (1985) *Sociology and School Knowledge*, London: Methuen.

Young, M. (1971) 'An approach to the study of curricula as socially organized knowledge', in Young, M. (Ed) *Knowledge and Control*, London: Collier Macmillan, pp. 19–46.

Chapter 10

Managing in Turbulent Times

Janet Ouston,
Policy Studies Management Development Centre, Institute of Education
University of London

Introduction

This chapter does not take the usual approach of most 'how to do it' books and merely offer its own prescription for 'managing change'. Readers who are familiar with several of these texts will notice two things: that they have very different perspectives and prescriptions from each other, and few have any doubts about the self-evident correctness of their own position. This chapter will not follow this pattern and offer yet another blueprint. It will present, and evaluate, a conceptual model which attempts to explain how these different approaches relate to each other, and how each might be particularly appropriate for different types of changes in different contexts.

Key issues for managers:

- What is your understanding of the organization you work in? Do you understand it as a rational organization where actions and outcomes are predictable?

- What is your understanding of the external context? Is it rapidly changing in unpredictable ways, or is it relatively stable?

- Do rational models fit your understanding of your school? Which of the models of change does your experience of being a manager in your particular school support?

- What is your attitude to risk and control? Are you comfortable with devolving management to your more junior colleagues — and to 'trying things out' — or do you feel that professional responsibility demands tighter control?

- What is your role in the clarification of values underpinning the school? Should managers decide values, or negotiate them with others?

It should be noted that 'managing change' has, in the past, been seen as something special, which occurs intermittently against a background of stability. Theorists of post-modernity (for example Harvey, 1990) argue that this is no longer the case. Decisions can no longer be made using rational frameworks to plan for, and implement, 'progress'. Harvey (p. 11) quotes Yeats to support this interpretation: 'Things fall apart; the centre cannot hold; mere anarchy is loosed upon the world'.

It is argued that the complexity of local and national organizations, and their dependence on rapidly changing international financial circumstances, makes long-term rational planning and control impossible. The British economy is inextricably linked with the economies of other parts of the world so that decisions about public expenditure are governed by factors outside national control. Harvey argues that in post-modern society time and space have become compressed, leaving us 'to withdraw into a kind of shell shocked, blasé, or exhausted silence' (p. 350). He argues that alternative responses can include denial, 'satisficing' (i.e. limiting one's interpretation and decision-making to a small part of the whole) or 'trying to ride the tiger of time space compression . . . and hopefully command it' (p. 351). He is not optimistic about the success of this final option. Post-modernists would argue that the rational interpretation of organizations, where actions and responses follow understood and predictable patterns, and where stability is its natural state, is no longer tenable. Rapid change is a regular part everyone's lives, including teachers, and occurs in response to external pressures and expectations, in addition to teachers' own decisions to improve the quality of teaching and learning offered to their students.

Change in education has major differences from change in other kinds of organization. Most changes in education in England and Wales in recent years have been imposed through direct government action, or indirect demands resulting from the 1988, and subsequent, education acts, the impact of examination league tables and the very detailed expectations set out in the Ofsted inspection handbooks. The interacting pressures of centrally imposed initiatives, have placed schools in a very different position to most commercial organizations. While they too experience pressures from the rapidly changing external environment, in the main, they have choices over how, what, and whether, to change some aspect of their practice while schools have far fewer choices. In reading about change written from non-educational perspectives these differences must be kept in mind.

Turbulence

Before moving on to look at the models, the concept of turbulence will be explored. Wallace and McMahon (1994) see turbulence as referring to both internal changes within organizations, and external changes in demands from their environments. As they point out, schools will have areas of turbulence and stability co-existing at the same time, but the balance may be more towards one than the other at different times. Lewin (1951), using systems theory, argued that organizational change could only occur in conditions of instability — he referred to stable organizations as being 'frozen', and that they had to be 'unfrozen' before change could occur. But a 'turbulent' internal and external environment suggests not merely pressure for change, but rapidly changing pressures with different levels of intensity and different areas of focus. There is also the implication that turbulence provokes unpredictable behaviour, and may lead to a lack of control or direction, which in its turn, may damage the organization's processes and outcomes.

Two key features in most rational analyses of change are whether the change is imposed, or chosen by school personnel, and whether the extent of the changes sought can be implemented directly, or require more widespread changes before the particular change can be introduced. Cuban (1988) distinguished between first and second order changes: first order change is about doing what we already do, but doing it differently. Second order, more complex, change demands changes in the organization first. Turbulent change might be defined as more second order changes than the organization can readily absorb.

Imposed change is often made more acceptable by developing or modifying what is required. Many schools 'domesticated' the National Curriculum through the process of introducing it: teachers took ownership of the changes during the implementation process. Indeed, one could argue that second order changes may make first order changes more psychologically acceptable.

It is important in any discussion of imposed change to consider who is imposing on whom. Senior management teams can choose to change, while at the same time imposing changes on their more junior colleagues. Whether teachers perceive that they have choice or not may depend on their role within the organization, and its internal management.

The outcome of the second issue concerning the potentially damaging effects of turbulence will depend on how the change is managed, on the expertise and previous experience of those leading and implementing the changes. Wallace and McMahon (1994) provide interesting case studies which set out the different approaches to managing change in primary schools.

Will Turbulence Continue?

By 1996 the pressure for change in education appeared to be diminishing: the National Curriculum had been revised, schemes of local management were established, and Ofsted's inspection practice was well known. It seemed possible that the pace of change had slowed slightly from that imposed during the previous five years. But with the election of a new government, which is clearly intending to intervene more directly in school and classroom practice (see the White Paper *Excellence in Schools*, DfEE, 1997), the external pressures for specific changes may be increasing. It is difficult to predict how these new policies will be received by schools, in contrast to the previous administration's approach which demanded changes in outcomes — through expected attainment on key stage tests, for example — but left schools to establish their own methods of meeting the targets. Similarly, the setting of school priorities, which has in the recent past been the school's responsibility within national guidelines, will increasingly require liaison with, and guidance from, the LEA. The proposed reinvigoration of the relationship between schools and LEAs may be very supportive, or it may be a potential source of tension and conflict and in itself create a more turbulent environment. The government's stated intention of 'intervention being in inverse proportion to success' (DfEE, 1997) may create more turbulence in some schools, and possibly in those least able to manage, or even to survive, it.

There has been considerable discussion in recent years about the use of new information and communication technologies in schools, and the extent to which these will revolutionize their work (Barber, 1996). The arguments centre around two key issues: do the new technologies have the potential to radically change teaching and learning, leading to the development of the 'virtual school'; and if they do can we (as a whole society) afford the costs of introducing and maintaining such an IT-rich environment? Clearly innovations like the Internet offer enhanced access to information, but will it lead to a radical transformation of learning or merely different, and perhaps better, ways of doing the same things? Barber argues that it will, but others (for example Cuban, 1986; Oppenheimer, 1997) are more cautious, seeing technology as being another tool to support the teacher and the student, but not a way of radically changing schools or learning.

Models of Managing Change

The models to be reviewed here are presented in order starting with those which assume a rational understanding of organizational dynamics, and linear and predictable relationships between management action and its outcomes. The individual models will not be described in detail.

Over the last ten years, writers on the management of change have progressed from assumptions of both rationality and linearity to models which assume neither. (See Wallace and McMahon, 1994, for a discussion of these issues.) These more recent approaches have not, however, yet made an impact on the expectations which the DfEE and Ofsted have of schools. They may find themselves undertaking several different planning processes at the same time for different purposes: for example, school development planning for Ofsted and flexible planning for their own management.

Alternative approaches to change in educational organizations will be presented in four broad categories as shown in *Figure 10.1*: the first group includes approaches which argue that change can be understood, and that there are predictable links between teachers' decisions and actions, and outcome. The second group stresses the importance of the meaning which participants develop to understand change and the third uses the notions of 'bounded rationality' and 'satisficing' (March and Simon, 1958) where decisions are made within a limited area to be 'good enough' rather than ideal. The fourth group of theorists in the main reject rationality and linearity because of the complexity of organizations and the unpredictability of the links between action and outcome. It should be noted that these groups of theories did not emerge in this time sequence: in the main the earliest theories to be discussed here are those in the middle groups. These were then rejected for the first group of rational and linear models, which are now being challenged by the fourth group writers who favour non-rational and non-linear models. This parallels the developments in theories about leadership explored in Chapter 3. As rational models are replaced by non-rational ones, personal and collective values take a higher profile. If one holds to scientific models of management, the key question is which management actions are most likely to lead to the desired outcome? Concern about values may be a minor issue. But once one moves to an understanding of organizations as complex and non-linear then values move to centre stage. If these are not made explicit, taken-for-granted values — and conflicts — will be powerful but lead to outcomes which no one desires.

Figure 10.1: *Alternative approaches to change*

rational models of organizations assumed linear relationships between action and outcome	**Group 1**
	a: school development planning (Hargreaves and Hopkins, 1991)
	b: planned change (Everard and Morris, 1996)
	c: strategic planning (Fidler, 1997)
	d: flexible planning (Wallace and McMahon, 1994)
	Group 2
	e: 'the meaning of change' (Fullan with Stiegelbauer, 1991)
less- and non-rational models assumed non-linear relationships between action and outcome	**Group 3**
	f: incremental planning (Lindblom, 1959)
	g: evolutionary planning (Louis and Miles, 1990)
	Group 4
	h: garbage can model (March and Olsen, 1976)
	j: 'change forces' (Fullan, 1993)
	k: chaos theory (Stacey, 1992; Maxcy, 1995)
	m: managing as a performing art (Vaill, 1991)

It will be argued that relatively limited changes in a non-turbulent environment are most appropriately managed using the approaches set out in *Group 1* while highly complex changes in a turbulent environment may be most appropriately managed using those set out in *Group 4*. Approaches set out in *Groups 2* and *3* are seen as intermediate, and appropriate for intermediate sets of changes and environments. As we move from (a) to (m) we move from assumptions of linearity and rationality, to assumptions of complexity, non-linearity and non-rationality. The move from model (a) to (m) could also be seen as a move from prescriptive models of change (what *ought* to be done) to descriptive models (what *is* done) although all the models in *Group 4* use description as a starting point for suggestions for action. The theorists included in *Figure 10.1* are chosen as widely read, and thought-provoking, examples of each approach, but others could have been included in their place.

School Development Planning

Towards the end of the 1980s (after the introduction of local management of schools in the Education Act, 1988) the concept of school development planning was introduced. Schools were encouraged, and later required, to prepare school development plans to guide their management (Hargreaves and Hopkins, 1991; MacGilchrist, Mortimore, Savage and Beresford, 1995). This is a rational and linear model of managing change, where most of the issues are seen to be readily grasped and where 'the correct' action is assumed to lead directly to a predictable outcome. (School development planning is discussed in more detail in Chapter 9)

Strategic Planning

Two major concerns have been raised about development planning as an approach to managing change. Fidler (1997) has argued that development plans take insufficient account of the charging pressures from the external environment, and of future likely change external to the school. This leads him to argue for strategic rather than development planning: he argues that the main difference between the two approaches is at the stage of analysis which is undertaken in preparation for writing the plan. This analysis should include an examination of relevant factors outside the school and consideration of the school and its future — often called 'environmental scanning' and 'scenario writing'. Everard and Morris (1996) offer a similar model of managing change, which draws on the work of Beckhard and Harris (1987).

Flexible Planning

Second, the traditional approach to development planning has been questioned by Wallace and McMahon (1994) who argue that the very rapid rate of change in schools leads successful managers to adopt a *flexible* approach to planning where plans are changed frequently in response to changing external events. This might be summed up by the comment 'We don't let the SDP get in the way of making, implementing and responding to, real change'. Both strategic planning and flexible planning are seen as essentially rational, and assume linear, if complex, links between management action and outcome. However, as Fidler (1997) has pointed out, flexible planning is inevitably reactive, and may be slower than is needed in a fast changing external world. School managers may be constantly trying to 'catch-up' with change, writing flexible plans for the past.

Personal Perspectives

Fullan with Stiegelbauer (1991), in their influential book *The New Meaning of Education Change*, moved away from the fully rational model by stressing the importance of participants' own creation of meaning in the implementation of change. Different participants may develop different meanings for the same change programme, leading them to act in different, and to the outside observer, unpredictable ways. When the purpose of an innovation is not clear to all, participants may develop their personal — and to them rational — 'false clarity' which will differ from person to person. This notion echoes that of Greenfield (Greenfield and Ribbins, 1993) who argued that organizations could only be understood subjectively, and that 'the organization' did not exist beyond its social construction. Much of Fullan with Stiegelbauer's discussion is based on change that has been chosen by schools rather than on the experience in England and Wales of imposed change. It is important to bear this in mind when considering their work as a model of change in English and Welsh schools: it is possible that there may be less 'false clarity' among teachers here when government-led initiatives are so widely publicized and discussed.

Fullan with Stiegelbauer (1991) proposed that change has four stages: initiation, implementation, continuation and outcomes. These are not linked in a simple, one-way, sequence, but assumes that there may be feedforward and feedback between each of the phases, for example implementation will affect continuation, and continuation will also affect implementation. This is potentially a very complex model of change, with each of these four phases interacting with the others. They argue that 'change is a process, not an event' (p. 49), and that it cannot be assumed that initiation and implementation will lead quite unproblematically to the desired out-comes. Like Wallace and McMahon (1994) they see the participants in educational change constantly assessing implementation and making adjustments as needed.

Incremental and Evolutionary Planning

The next group of change management theories can be seen in the context of Weick's notion of schools as 'loosely coupled systems' (Weick, 1976). Teachers are seen as working relatively independently of each other in their own classrooms, having little direct impact on other teachers' practices. Teachers are not constantly supervised as other workers are, and diversity has often been seen as a positive outcome of teachers' professionalism and relative autonomy. But there are clearly questions to ask about the extent to which schools in England and Wales have become more tightly-coupled in the last ten years. The introduction of a national curriculum has probably led to less freedom for individual teachers, and school-based management and the typical move to tighter internal line-management may have led to schools being more tightly-coupled systems than they were. This point will be revisited later in the discussion of the third group of theories.

Two theories are presented as being typical of those in the middle ground between rationality and non-rationality, but both assume that there is a linear link between action and outcome, at least in the short-term. Lindblom's (1959) incre-mental planning model has similarities to Wallace and McMahon's (1994) model of flexible planning. Lindblom argued that planning decisions were generally made incrementally, using what he described as 'the science of muddling through'. While this might be interpreted as a disparaging description, it can be argued that incre-mental approaches to organizational change are more likely to be successful in a complex environment: decisions are made rationally as those which are most likely to *contribute* to achieving longer-term objectives. But the whole chain of actions to achieve these is not planned in advance. A good metaphor here is sailing in a rough sea: sailors will know what they wish to achieve but will make decisions incre-mentally about the direction to take at any particular instant based on experience and intuition. This process is repeated until the goal is achieved. (A similar approach has been developed by Deming (1992) as the plan–do–study–act cycle, which will be discussed later in this chapter.)

Evolutionary planning for change (Louis and Miles, 1990) has similarities with incremental planning. This approach argues for the importance of developing shared aims and values, but that individuals will each, in their own short-term decision-making, contribute to the collective outcome. These outcomes will be responsive to external and internal changes through the collective responsiveness of individual decision makers.

Non-rational, Non-linear Models

Moving on to explore the models of educational change included in *Group 4*, these do not assume rational organizational models, or that there are linear and predict-able relationships between management action and outcome. It is striking that Fullan's two books on educational change are so different in their approach (Fullan with Stiegelbauer, 1991 and Fullan, 1993). As he says in the preface to the later book:

> We are going to end up debunking myths, exposing half truths, and juxtaposing things that do not normally go together. I will be calling into question vision and strategic planning, site based management, strong leadership, accountability and assessment schemes, collegiality and consensus and other favorites of the day. (Fullan, 1993, p. vii)

This is a truly radical agenda with post-modern overtones, but one that is echoed by all the writers in this category. This agenda is both intellectually exciting but sometimes difficult to grasp: trying to think coherently about non-rationality and non-linearity is very challenging and often feels paradoxical. How do we 'manage the unknowable' (Stacey, 1992)? But before exploring these ideas in more depth we will start by discussing the 'garbage-can' model of March and Olsen (1976). This is a descriptive model of how decisions are made in complex educational organizations, where decisions are seen as resulting from 'the idiosyncratic and illogical inter-actions in a "garbage-can" between four variables . . . problems, . . . solutions, . . . participants . . . and choice opportunities' (Wallace and McMahon, 1994, page 23). Wallace and McMahon question how such organizations survive, but it may be that the garbage-can approach enables evolutionary planning to take place. Provided that there is some agreement about the aims and purposes of the organization, the apparently uncoordinated actions of individuals may lead to appropriate action.

Each of the writers in *Group 4* is concerned with the facilitation and use of patterns which emerge within the unpredictability they see in complex organizations. They assume that there are no simple linear links between causes and effects: that actions may have very varying, and unpredictable, outcomes because of complex chains of organizational processes. Theorists who take a rational approach would try to understand these by hypothesizing complex contingencies — if action 'a' happens in context 'b' then 'c' will result and this will ultimately, through a complex chain of actions, contexts and outcomes, lead to outcome 'g'. The theorists in *Group 4* deny that this level of predictability can ever be achieved. All come to similar conclusions: that modern organizations are too complex to explain in this way and argue that the most effective management model is 'the learning organisation' (Senge, 1990). In the learning organization decisions are taken at all levels; team work and diversity is encouraged and valued; conflicts and mistakes are used as part of the organizational learning process. But these are set within a culture of explicit and shared values. Fullan (1993) sees the new role of the headteacher not as a strong leader but as a leader of the collective learning who articulates the school's developing values. He argues that 'vision and strategic planning come later' and that 'premature visions and planning (can) blind' (p. 21). He contrasts this to the strategic planning approach and summarizes Beckhard and Pritchard's (1992) views of leaders 'creating and setting the vision, communicating the vision, building commitment to the vision, and organising people and what they do so that they are aligned to the vision' (p. 29). There is a clear conflict between these approaches.

In recent years 'chaos theory' (Gleick, 1987; Maxcy, 1995) has been a powerful influence on the development of non-linear approaches to the conceptualization of organizations. Chaos theory was developed to explain the regular but unpredictable nature of many natural phenomena, and the way in which recognizable 'bounded' patterns emerge in such complex, and apparently random systems. The usual example given of a chaotic system is the world-wide weather, where recognizable patterns of weather occur, but where the system is too complex, with too many complex internal interactions, to permit any predictions other than those in the very short term. Wheatley's writing on organizational leadership from a chaos theory perspective has been very influential in translating chaos theory from the 'hard' to the social sciences (Wheatly, 1992).

Fullan (1993) acknowledges the influence of Stacey's work (1992) on 'managing the unknowable' on his changed thinking about the nature of change in education. Stacey dismisses long-term visions and plans: 'a shared vision of a future state must be a dangerous illusion' (p. 23). He says that

> . . . effective management focuses on ever-changing agendas of strategic issues. These agendas consist of multiple challenges, stretching aspirations and ambiguous issues. The challenges, aspirations and issues all arise out of ill-structured and conflicting changes occurring in the here and now but having long-term widespread consequences. Such a vibrant agenda of issues means that the organisation does not hitch its future to any one development alone. From all this, it is only with hindsight that we can detect a 'vision' or describe a plan. (p. 23)

He goes on to argue that 'shared cultures block an organisation's ability to handle live strategic issue agendas' and that what is needed is 'spontaneous, self-organising learning groups of managers, tackling conflict, engaging in dialogue and publicly testing assertions that are vital to the handling of strategic issues' (p. 24). He sees strategy as emerging from the learning which takes place in these circumstances, and through micropolitical interaction. 'Continuing success flows from non equilibrium, creative interaction with the environment, not adaptive equilibrium that simply comes from building on existing strengths' (p. 25).

Chaos theory also acted as the starting point for Gunter (1997), who argues against what she calls the 'quick-fix ring binder' approach to education management with solutions to management problems available off-the-shelf. Using chaos theory as a context she argues for the empowerment that will come from professional reflection and reflexivity. This echoes Stacey's emphasis on group learning, and on the empowerment of staff in the learning organization.

Maxcy (1995) in his critique of chaos theory, and in an overstatement from the UK perspective, says that 'chaos thinking has become a full-blown theory of education in a few short years'. He is critical of its tendency to ignore individuals, seeing them as merely interchangeable parts of the whole system. He is also critical of its ambition to become yet another 'grand theory' which explains everything, and the rapid transitions chaos theorists make from physics to organizational analysis. The opposite view is taken by Snyder, Acker-Hocevar and Wolf (1995) who argue for the integration of chaos theory and quality management: '. . . the patterns that emerged from the (research) interviews reinforce the utility of quality as a mental model for guiding change; and chaos as a theory for grounding their efforts' (p. 30). But they would both agree that much of conventional educational management is too firmly rooted in a belief in, and search for, rational, orderly organizations and fails to grasp the challenge and excitement of the unpredictable and disorderly.

Maxcy (1995) concludes by dismissing the value of chaos theory as an approach to understanding and improving education and argues for 'moral artistry', for values-based education and educational organizations.

Our final writer takes us further into understanding organizations and organizational change through values and metaphors. Vaill (1991) writes about rafting in a raging river, the 'permanent white water', and about baseball. He describes a game that is just like conventional baseball, with one change to the rules: whenever the ball is in the air anyone can move any of the bases — anywhere. Does this describe the school management game too? He goes on to discuss whether this game would be played in a similar way to the conventional game, or whether we would develop 'a completely different concept of what "playing well" means' (p. 3). His analysis makes many similar points to Stacey (1992) and concludes that in turbulence we have to work collectively smarter — by working together; reflectively smarter — so that we understand and share new meanings and understandings; and spiritually smarter — by understanding what we are doing and the moral values and purposes that underlie action.

Conclusions

This chapter has reviewed the very different approaches to managing organizations in changing circumstances. It started with the now 'traditional' approach in schools to school development planning, and moved away from rational and linear models of organizations to the heady world of chaos theory and 'managing by metaphor'. It has tried to show that these different approaches do not merely reflect fickleness on the part of the writers but can be placed in a conceptual framework. Two important questions remain: which of these groups of models do we use when faced with a practical management problem, and is it possible to combine the various models into one super-model that will provide guidance in all circumstances? At the beginning of this chapter it was argued that we moved from *Group 1* to *Group 4* as the organization being managed was conceptualized as more complex, and less rational. This is an important distinction. It is possible to write a traditional school development plan to manage change over the coming academic year provided that we see the school as a rational organization in a relatively stable environment, and the outcomes of management action as predictable. The extent to which this is a worthwhile model will depend on whether these assumptions are justified and also on the level of detail in the plan. A very detailed process-based plan (how are things to be done) would be more vulnerable to lack of rationality, linearity, stability and predictability than a much broader brush statement of aims and purposes.

It would be argued that the manager would move from *Group 1* approaches, to those in *Group 4*, according to the complexity of the organizational dynamics relating to the particular innovations. King (1997), using Deming's (1992) ideas, has argued that highly complex organizations can be made more 'manageable' by very short-term cycles of evaluation, action and review. He has demonstrated that frequent use of the plan–do–study–act cycle to understand the processes of complex systems allows us to intervene to ameliorate the damaging impact of chaos without removing its positive, creative aspects. This is rather similar to Fullan's notion of 'ready, fire, aim' (p. 31) where the doing (firing) creates information from which the aims can be developed. This is very different to the traditional approach of setting aims first.

The chapter ends with three quotations from an experienced headteacher (Mary Marsh) which demonstrate this approach:

> . . . knowing how important it is that you try things even if it isn't what you end up wanting to do in the longer term. What you've learnt from trying is of benefit when you actually come to taking things forward. If you wait to arrive at the perfect solution by discussion, debate, and (waiting for) somebody else to tell you, I think you make very slow progress. So I very much wanted to get on and do things, and try to make debate and discussion focused on particular issues in defined time spans . . . (Ouston, 1997, p. 142)

> So what it is that you are trying to do often is much less important than how you're trying to do it, and that's the bit you need to get right. Yes, you've got to set clear targets and objectives, but shouldn't spend weeks developing elaborate ones. Keep it snappy, short, focused, and get on with it. Do it and review it. 'Is it working? No, it isn't. What do we do next?' So it's much more immediate and not so large scale. (Ouston, 1997, p. 143)

This approach to managing in turbulence uses rational approaches to small parts of the school system for relatively short periods of time. As Mary Marsh stresses, it is set in a context of trust, openness and collaboration:

> In terms of values I am passionately committed to openness and trust — and being direct . . . I'm very aware of how vulnerable people's confidence, and their trust, actually is.
> . . . I'm looking to do things with other people, rather than to them or for them — that's fundamental. (Ouston, 1997, p. 142)

References

BARBER, M. (1996) *The Learning Game: Arguments for an Educational Revolution*, London: Gollancz.

BECKHARD, R. and HARRIS, R.T. (1987) *Organizational Transitions: Managing Complex Change*, (2nd edition), New York: Addison Wesley.

BECKHARD, R. and PRITCHARD, W. (1992) *Changing the Essence*, San Francisco: Jossey-Bass.

CUBAN, L. (1986) *Teachers and Machines: The Classroom Use of Technology since 1920*, New York: Teachers College Press.

CUBAN, L. (1988) 'A fundamental puzzle of school reform', *Phi Delta Kappan*, **70**, 5, pp. 341–344.

DEMING, W.E. (1992) *The New Economics*, Cambridge, Ma: MIT.

DEPARTMENT FOR EDUCATION AND EMPLOYMENT (1997) *Excellence in Schools*, London: HMSO.

EVERARD, K.B. and MORRIS, G. (1996) *Effective School Management*, (3rd edition) London: Paul Chapman Publishing.

FIDLER, B. (1997) 'Strategic management' in FIDLER, B., RUSSELL, S. and SIMKINS, T. (Eds) *Choices for Self-managing Schools*, London: Paul Chapman Publishing (pp. 86–104).

FIDLER, B. (1997) Personal communication.

FULLAN, M. with STIEGELBAUER, S. (1991) *The New Meaning of Educational Change*, London, Cassell.

FULLAN, M. (1993) *Change Forces: Probing the Depths of Educational Reform*, London: Falmer Press.

GLEICK, J. (1987) *Chaos Theory*, London: Penguin Books.

GREENFIELD, T.B. and RIBBINS, P. (1993) *Greenfield on Educational Administration: Towards a Humane Science*, London: Routledge.

GUNTER, H. (1997) *Rethinking Education: The Consequences of Jurassic Management*, London: Cassell.

HARGREAVES, D. and HOPKINS, D. (1991) *The Empowered School*, London: Cassell.

HARVEY, D. (1990) *The Condition of Post-modernity: An Enquiry into the Origins of Cultural Change*, Oxford: Blackwell.

KING, D. (1997) PhD dissertation in preparation, Institute of Education, University of London.

KOSKO, B. (1994) *Fuzzy Thinking: The New Science of Fuzzy Logic*, London: Harper Collins.

LEWIN, K. (1951) *Field Theory in Social Science*, New York: Harper and Row.

LOUIS, K.S. and MILES, M.B. (1992) *Improving the Urban Highschool*, London: Cassell.

LINDBLOM, C.E. (1959) 'The science of muddling through', *Public Administration Review*, **19**, 2, pp. 79–88.

MACGILCHRIST, B., MORTIMORE, P., SAVAGE, J. and BERESFORD, C. (1995) *Planning Matters: The Impact of Development Planning in Primary Schools*, London: Paul Chapman Publishing.

MARCH, J.G. and OLSEN, J.P. (eds) (1976) *Ambiguity and Choice in Organization*, Bergen, Norway: Universitets forlaget.

MARCH, J.G. and SIMON, H.A. (1958) *Organizations*, New York: John Wiley.

MAXCY, S.J. (1995) *Democracy, Chaos and the New School Order*, California: Corwin Press.

OPPENHEIMER, T. (1997) 'The computer delusion', *The Atlantic Monthly*, **280**, 1, pp. 45–62 (July 1997) (http://www.theatlantic.com).

OUSTON, J. (1997) 'Mary Marsh in conversation with Janet Ouston', in RIBBINS, P. (Ed) *Leaders and Leadership in the School, College and University*, London: Cassell (pp. 131–44).

OWENS, R.G. (1995) *Organizational Behavior in Education*, Boston: Allyn and Bacon.

SENGE, P. (1990) *The Fifth Discipline*, New York: Doubleday.

SNYDER, K.J., ACKER-HOCEVAR, M. and WOLF, K.M. (1995) 'Chaos theory as a lens for advancing quality schooling'. Paper given to the British Education Management and Administration Society Annual Conference, Oxford, September 1995.

STACEY, R. (1992) *Managing Chaos*, London: Kogan Page. (Published in the USA as *Managing the Unknowable*, San Francisco: Jossey-Bass.)

VAILL, P.B. (1991) *Managing as a Performing Art: New Ideas for a World of Chaotic Change*, San Francisco: Jossey-Bass.

WALLACE, M. and MCMAHON, A. (1994) *Planning for Change in Turbulent Times*, London: Cassell.

WEICK, K.E. (1976) 'Educational organizations as loosely-coupled systems', *Administrative Science Quarterly*, **21**, 1, pp. 1–19.

WHEATLEY, M.J. (1992) *Leadership and the New Science: Learning about Organization from an Orderly Universe*, San Francisco: Berrett Koehler.

WILSON, D.C. (1992) *A Strategy of Change: Concepts and Controversies in the Management of Change*, London: Routledge.

Index